BRAZIL
War on Children

Gilberto Dimenstein

Introduction by Jan Rocha

This book is dedicated to the National Movement of Street
Children for its lonely, silent, but courageous work.

LATIN AMERICA BUREAU
Research, publishing and education on Latin America and the Caribbean

First published in 1991 by the Latin America Bureau (Research and Action) Ltd, 1
Amwell Street, London EC1R 1UL

A CIP catalogue record for this book is available from the British Library

ISBN 0 906156 62 9 PBK
ISBN 0 906156 63 7 HBK

Written by Gilberto Dimenstein
Introduction by Jan Rocha
Translated by Chris Whitehouse
Edited by Duncan Green

Photographs by Paula Simas
Cover photograph by Susan Cunningham
Cover design by Andy Dark

Typeset, printed and bound by Russell Press, Nottingham NG7 3HN
Trade distribution in UK by Central Books, 99 Wallis Road, London E9 5LN
Distribution in North America by Monthly Review Press, 122 West 27th Street, New
York, NY 10001

Printed on recycled, straw-based paper.

Edinburgh University Library

RETURN BY

	1 9 MAR 1998	
23 MAR 94 / 12. SEP	2 2 APR 1998	
01. 12. 94	- 5 APR 1999 / 2 3 NOV 1999	
2 2 MAR 1995	1 7 FEB 2000	
26. 07.	1 6 MAR 2000	
29. 11.	1 3 APR 2000	
	2 8 JUL 2000	
1 0 JAN 1996		
	2 3 JUL 2002	
2 5 JAN 1996	2 0 NOV 2002	
1 2 NOV 1996	2 2 IAN 2013	

FINES RATE:

1. 10p per volume per day for NORMAL loans (6 wks).
2. 50p per volume per day for RECALLED books.

Contents

Glossary

CBIA	*Fundaçâo Centro Brasileiro para a Infância e Adolescência* Central Brazilian Foundation for Infancy and Adolescence
CIEPS	*Centros Integrado de Educaçao Popular* Integrated Centres for Popular Education
	Comissão Justiça e Paz Catholic Church Justice and Peace Commission
	favela shanty town
FEBEM	*Fundaçao do Bem-Estar do Menor* Foundation for Child Welfare (state-run)
FUNABEM	*Fundaçao Nacional do Bem-Estar do Menor* National Foundation for Child Welfare
IBASE	*O Instituto Brasileiro de Análises Sociais e Econômicas* Brazilian Institute for Social and Economic Analysis
IBGE	*Instituto Brasileiro de Geografia e Estatistica* the official Statistics Office
IML	*Instituto Médico Legal* Legal Medical Institute
	Juizado de Menores Juvenile Courts
	justiceiros 'avengers', death squad gunmen
	Ministério da Criança Ministry of the Child
MNMMR	*Movimento Nacional de Meninos e Meninas de Rua* National Movement of Street Children
	Movimento pela Vida Movement for Life

OAB	*Orden de Advogados Brasileiros* Brazilian Lawyers' Order
OPM	*Organizaçao Pena de Morte* Death Penalty Organisation
PDC	*Partido Democrata Cristão* Christian Democrat Party
PT	*Partido dos Trabalhadores* Workers' Party
PTB	*Partido Trabalhista Brasileira* Brazilian Labour Party
	Pastoral do Menor da Diocese de Duque de Caxias Church Pastoral Service for Children, Duque de Caxias
	SOS Criança SOS Children

Newspapers

Correio Brasiliense
Folha de São Paulo
Jornal do Brasil
Jornal do Comercio
L'Express
O Globo
O Povo

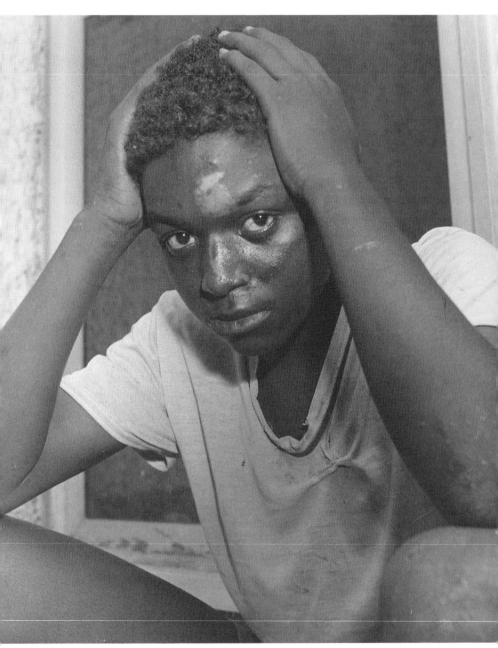

Too frightened to go to hospital, Recife.

Preface

Recife, 11 o'clock on a warm Wednesday night, 17 January 1990, and Paula Simas, photographer, arrives at the cafe. I expected her to be hungry because she only had a sandwich and a glass of lemonade for lunch. She puts her camera on the chair to her side. She seems disheartened and has a far-away look in her eyes. She hardly touches her food. I know why: she has just been doing the rounds to take more photos for this book. That night had been especially hard for her. While she was taking photos, a young girl clutched her tightly and said in an imploring voice, 'Please, take me away from here.'

One of the children she photographed told her that he would only find peace of mind when he finally got a bullet in the head. A few yards away, another boy told her he had been hit in the leg by a police bullet. He was afraid to go to the hospital because he knew they would hand him over to the *Juizado de Menores*, the juvenile court. If this happened, he told Paula, he would fall into the hands of the death squads and that would be the end of him. I suppose it was quite natural that anybody with any feelings should not feel hungry.

During the visits that we made to six of Brazil's largest cities in January and February, 1990, we came across many similar situations. It was impossible not to be affected by the stories we heard of the torture, ill-treatment and murder of children. The drama of the children's testimony seemed to have a physical effect on us. It was not just a question of going off your food. At night, back at the hotel after a day's work, I felt an obsessive desire to take a long, hot bath. We often spent the day in the sun and many of the places we visited in the shanty towns stank, but I needed a bath not so much to get rid of the sweat or the smell. It was more a need to wash away all that I had heard; a vague, useless attempt to expunge from my memory words I did not want to hear, like trying to shake the dust from my clothes.

Gilberto Dimenstein

The above passage is an extract from the preface to *A Guerra dos Meninos*, the original Brazilian edition of Gilberto Dimenstein's book, published in São Paulo in 1990.

BRAZIL

1 ACRE	9 RIO GRANDE DO NORTE	17 MATO GROSSO DO SUL
2 AMAZONAS	10 PARAIBA	18 GOIAS
3 RORAIMA	11 PERNAMBUCO	19 MINAS GERAIS
4 PARA	12 ALAGOAS	20 ESPIRITO SANTO
5 AMAPA	13 SERGIPE	21 RIO DE JANEIRO
6 MARANHAO	14 BAHIA	22 SAO PAULO
7 PIAUI	15 RONDONIA	23 PARANA
8 CEARA	16 MATO GROSSO	24 SANTA CATARINA
		25 RIO GRANDE DO SUL

National border   ‐‐‐‐‐‐‐‐
State borders   ‐‐‐‐‐‐‐‐‐‐‐‐‐‐

km   1000   scale

Introduction

At least once a week, late at night, a woman comes to my door to ask for food, clothing and money. With her are four or five small children, tired, sometimes shivering in the rain, sometimes crying with cold and hunger. They carry bags and bundles, the product of the night's begging. The journey home to their *favela* (shanty town) in a São Paulo suburb must take at least an hour by bus.

On every visit the woman has a new problem to report. The water company has cut off her water supply because she has not paid the bill. The oldest boy wants to go to school but has no shoes. The oldest girl is going to start school — but they have given her a list of things she must take — notebooks, crayons, ruler, eraser, scissors — how can she afford them? The floods have swept away their shack and now they are homeless. The local administration has given them a piece of land and they have the bricks to build a new home, but they cannot afford the tiles for the roof. Instead, they have had to use wooden boards, but the rain comes in and makes everything damp. One of the boys got rheumatism and is now in hospital.

'I can't wait until they're a bit older and can go out to work', says the mother, who left her alcoholic husband behind when she came to the city. The children are beautiful, but they all have sad eyes.

In São Paulo, Brazil's largest and wealthiest city, ten per cent of the population, over one million people, now live in shanty towns. Another three million live in *cortiços* — collective dwellings which are usually large old houses divided up into tiny cubicles, one for each family. Up to 40 or 50 families share one bathroom, cooking and washing facilities.

In other cities the proportion of people living in *favelas* or substandard housing is even higher, and numbers are increasing.

In 1987, 20 families lived in wooden huts under a road flyover near my home. Now there are 200 families squeezed into a space less than 400 metres long beneath the flyover's concrete arch.

Poverty in Brazil is growing. Never has there been such a concentration of income. The richest ten per cent of Brazil's 150 million people earn over half of the national income (53.2 per cent). The poorest ten per cent receive less than one per cent (0.6 per cent).

The last official income survey in 1988 showed that 54 per cent of Brazil's children and adolescents live in families earning less than US$35 per month. Diarrhoea is the main cause of death of children under two, while 350,000 children under five die every year. In terms of per capita income Brazil has fallen from over US$2,000 to US$1,869 according to the *Instituto Brasileiro de Geografia e Estatistica*, the official Statistics Office (IBGE). and its infant mortality rate, 85 per 1,000, is much worse than in many poorer countries. In South America only Peru and Bolivia have a higher rate.

There are an estimated 25 million deprived children in Brazil, and of these between seven and eight million are on the streets. Only a minority are totally on their own — orphaned, abandoned or without any contact with their parents. Most maintain some contact, however tenuous, with their family. On the streets, home is a shop doorway, a bench in a square, a hot-air duct outside a restaurant, a bonfire on the beach, the steps of a railway station. Bed is a piece of cardboard, an old blanket, newspapers. Some sleep alone, others huddle together for warmth or protection. They never know when they might be woken up by a policeman's boot, a jet of cold water from a street-cleaning truck, or even a bullet from a vigilante group or gun-happy officer of the law.

Violence can also come from older children:

'One night I found an eight-year-old boy in the rubbish tip. The older boys had knifed him and thrown him there. I took him to hospital but next day he was back at the station', says Geraldo, a railway policeman at Rio's Central Station.

During the day, the street children's main concern is survival — food. To get it they beg, pick pockets, steal from shops, mug tourists, look after parked cars, shine shoes, or search litter bins. Frequently glue takes the place of food. They sniff it from paper bags and for a few glorious moments forget who or where they are.

'I sniffed a lot yesterday and then I dreamt of a school where we could learn ballet, the *capoeira* dance, reading and writing. School is the best thing in the world. I'm always dreaming about it,' says a young prostitute in Salvador. 'We sniff glue to forget our hunger. It changes our minds and makes us forget tons of things like discrimination. We can't get on a bus because people think we're going to steal,' adds a 12 year old in Rio.

A survey among street children in São Paulo showed that 'the more deficient their relations were with their families and school, the more they used drugs'. Out of 119 children aged six to 17, 45 per cent were classified as 'heavy drug users', using up to three different drugs every day, including glue, marijuana, alcohol and tobacco. Cocaine is a small but growing addition, while the incidence of AIDS among street children is also growing because of shared needles.

The street can seem attractive to children who at home are unwanted, battered and hungry. 'On the street it's better than at home', says a ten-year-old girl who sleeps on the steps of the municipal theatre in Rio. 'Here if you want money, you arrange it, that's life. Sometimes a pervert comes and asks us to go behind the theatre with him, but I've never gone.'

An eight year old who lives in a children's refuge in Rio called the Boys' Republic says, 'I live here because my stepfather doesn't like me. He drinks *cachaça* (sugar-cane rum) and rows with my mother. He used to hit me, pull my arm, pinch me. Here it's good. I'd only go and live with my mother if she didn't have my stepfather there.'

Some came from a small town or village in the interior, looking for work. 13-year-old Rosilene came to Rio with her older sister, but could not find a job and ended up on Copacabana beach, living under some trees with a group of others. Shy, humble, she seems bewildered.

Fear is a constant companion. In Fortaleza where the number has grown by half in three years, a survey found that their age is lower, more of them are illiterate and they are afraid of the police, bigger boys, the Juvenile Welfare Department, rapists, municipal inspectors who carry out blitzes on street sellers, thieves, and the traffic, in that order.

Street children often end up exploited by adults who transform them into professional criminals. Charles Dickens would recognise the scene in the old centre of Salvador where a band of 30 boys aged eight to 16 steal watches, cameras and handbags, preferably from women, old people and tourists, and bring their loot back to the house of a man called Dudua. In exchange he gives them a place to sleep, supplies them with drugs, glue to sniff, and gives them affection. Where it differs from *Oliver Twist* is that policemen also exploit the children, demanding money and stolen watches in exchange for letting them go free.

A few escape via the projects that volunteers and non-governmental organisations have set up in many cities. What must be as hard to bear as the fear and the hunger is the hostility and indifference that street children face from the general public. Brazilians are warm and hospitable, and they love children, but most of them do not see street children as children. What they see in these ragged, dirty kids, drugged or lively, cheeky or sad, is a threat. A threat to their property, a threat to their lives. That is why a few years ago in the centre of São Paulo a lawyer savagely kicked and stamped a 13-year-old boy called Jesus to death when he grabbed a woman's gold necklace. A crowd stood round him watching and egging him on. Only two young office girls protested at the brutal act.

In Salvador thousands of children live in the *palafitas* — shacks built on stilts over the water. The *O Globo* newspaper described their lives:

'They live in miserable shacks surrounded by sewer effluent disgorged in the area. They suffer from dysentery, scabies and skin diseases. Most of them do not go to school. Two thousand families live here with about 10,000 children. The children have to learn to look after themselves, from the moment they begin to walk. The first and fundamental lesson is about balance. They have to be able to walk along the narrow walkways of rotting planks. Any stumble can be fatal. Despite their agility, accidents are frequent. A few days ago a 10-year-old boy lost his balance when flying a kite and fell on to a stake under the water. He survived but had 51 stitches. Another boy fell and was electrocuted on the wires that pass under the planks.

Their parents work as maids, labourers, or do odd jobs, but there are also many unemployed, alcoholics, prostitutes and petty criminals. There are three crèches and three state primary schools which have hardly had any lessons this year because of teachers' strikes. "So that my two oldest could study, I had to withdraw the two youngest ones from school. Even then, I still had to cut down on food to buy their books," said one mother. Some families have 14 children.'

Most of these families have come to Salvador from rural areas looking for work. In desperation some families end up prostituting their own daughters in exchange for food. A local judge said girls as young as seven work in the red light zone. In Fortaleza, the Ceará capital, the director of the state juvenile welfare institute was quoted by an international human rights organisation as saying, 'Child prostitution has reached an unbearable level in Ceará. Parents hire out their daughters in exchange for food. There are brothels that specialise in offering 12-year-old virgins for tourists and special clients.'

Girl prostitutes told of being sent back by their own mothers if they came home without money to buy food. Others said that policemen took their money and sometimes forced them to have sex. There are said to be 500,000 under-age girl prostitutes in Brazil. The age of consent is 18.

For children who remain in rural areas life can be equally tough. A reporter for *Jornal do Brasil* described Christmas for young boys working in sugar-cane fields in Terra Nova, Bahia state. As there was no work, they got no food. Fourteen-year-old Manoel Luís said, 'I haven't got food or clothes or shoes. How can I have Christmas?' 10-year-old Josué Geraldo, the oldest of six children in a family fleeing the drought, had never been to school. The boys help their fathers and older brothers cut four tons of cane a day — a quota which earned them a monthly wage of about US$50. From this sum, the plantation deducted amounts for food and accommodation. Food consisted of rice, beans and cassava flour, sometimes with dried meat and they lived in derelict houses.

The agriculture workers' union reckons there are 2,000 children working in these conditions in the sugar-cane fields. 'In 1888 a slave cost so many tons of sugar, but today these children cost the sugarmill nothing,' says a union official. Since the sugar-cane industry in the Northeast is archaic, some argue that modernization is the answer, yet thousands of miles west of Bahia in the Eastern Amazon development area known as Grande Carajas, planned around the world's biggest iron ore deposit, financed by the European Community and the World Bank, 12 and 13-year-old boys work a ten-hour day in a hole in the ground, making charcoal. They work on the edge of a giant sawmill set up with government incentives and a ten-year tax holiday, designed to bring progress and employment to the area.

Life in a *favela*

Thirty years ago, Carolina Maria de Jesus described her daily life in a diary that became a best-selling book, *Beyond all Pity*.

–'Many people in the *favela* don't have warm clothing. When one has shoes he won't have a coat. I choke up watching the children walk in the mud. It seems that some new people have arrived in the *favela*. They are ragged with undernourished faces. They improvised a shack. It hurts me to see so much pain, reserved for the working class. I stared at my new companion in misfortune. She looked at the *favela* with its mud and sickly children. It was the saddest look I'd ever seen. Perhaps she has no more illusions. She had given her life over to misery.

What I revolt against is the greed of men who squeeze other men as if they were squeezing oranges...

Today the children are only going to get hard bread and beans with *farinha* (cassava flour) to eat. I'm so tired that I can't even stand up. I'm cold. Thank God we're not starving. Today, He is helping me. I'm confused and don't know what to do. I'm walking from one side to the other because I can't stand being in a shack as bare as this. A house that doesn't have a fire in the stove is so sad! And pots boiling on the fire also serve as decoration. It beautifies a place.

I went to Dona Nené. She was in the kitchen. What a marvellous sight! She was cooking chicken, meat and macaroni. She grated *half* a cheese to put on the macaroni! She gave me some *polenta* with chicken. It's been ten years ... I almost didn't know what it was.

The smell of the food in Dona Nené's house was so pleasant that tears streamed out of my eyes, because I felt so sorry for my children. They would have loved those delicacies ...

José Carlos came home with a bag of biscuits he'd found in the garbage. When I saw him eating things out of the trash I thought: and if it's been poisoned? Children can't stand hunger. The biscuits were delicious. I ate them thinking of the proverb: he who enters the dance must dance. And as I also was hungry I ate.

More new people arrived in the *favela*. They are shabby and walk bent over with their eyes on the ground as if doing penance for their misfortune of living in an ugly place. A place where you can't plant one flower to breathe its perfume ... the only perfume that comes from the *favela* is from rotting mud, excrement and whisky.'

Carolina Maria de Jesus, *Beyond All Pity*, Earthscan, 1990

Carolina Maria de Jesus wrote her book 30 years ago, but it could have been today. There is a housing deficit of at least ten million homes in Brazil, yet even when new homes are built, low-income families cannot afford them. For political reasons low-income homes are built only for sale, not for rent. 'House owners do not go in for revolution', the director of a housing programme once told me.

Most of Brazil's street children probably began life in a *favela* in São Paulo, Rio, Recife, Belém, or one of the other big cities. There are now 1,600 *favelas* in São Paulo alone, crammed into unwanted public areas — steep hillsides, along the banks of streams, under bridges and flyovers. Then there are the *loteamentos*, the settlements; either the result of illegal occupations of private and public property or the division of a piece of land into miniscule plots, which are sold to families and on which they build their homes.

Seventy-five per cent of Brazil's 150 million people now live in urban areas. There are over 20 cities with more than a million people, and Rio and São Paulo are among the five largest cities in the world. Brazil's great cities sprawl unplanned. Unplanned? Not according to the architects of São Paulo's City Planning Department who analysed the growth of their city:

'Far from representing the absence of planning, the periphery model [of *favelas*] responds to a strategy of maximum capitalist accumulation. It enables the settlement of large contingents of people in areas that are bare of anything.' The settlers have to do everything with their own hands, build their own homes, thus 'reducing to a minimum the need for investment in housing and infrastructure either by the public or private sector.'

The exodus from the land to the cities began in the 1950s when the car industry came to São Paulo and Brazil embarked on a crash industrialisation programme to end its dependence on imported manufactured goods. This import substitution programme reached its peak under the generals during the 21-year-long military regime from 1964-85. The policy turned Brazil into a land of migrants, families uprooted in search of work, food, health, gold, survival. Many of them do not move of their own accord, but are driven off their land by land grabbers, enclosures for cattle ranches, hydroelectric projects, mechanisation, violence, drought. Brazil has the most extreme concentration of land ownership in the world — as great as the concentration of income. The subsidies and incentives poured into the hands of ranchers, whether individuals or companies, Brazilian or multinational, have fuelled the concentration. Every government since 1964 has promised land reform and distributed a few land titles to the poor, but the large landowners' lobby has proved too powerful in Brasília and hired gunmen have systematically killed union leaders who fought for it.

In any case, say the architects in *São Paulo: Crisis and Change* (*São Paulo: Crise e Mudança*, Editora Brasiliense, 1991), the military wanted people to move to the cities where they were more easy to control and could provide the cheap labour needed for the generals' industrialisation programme. 'The network of cities reflects the military government's urban project. Its key concept is national integration to complete the occupation and unification of the country as a capitalist urban-industrial territory.' Long highway networks reached inland from the coast and then penetrated Brazil's vast interior. New industrial infrastructure — steelworks, aluminium plants, petrochemical plants, ports, bridges and hydroelectric dams — galvanised the economy. All this was financed by a concentration of funds and taxes in the hands of central government and the internationalisation of the economy (the beginning of Brazil's astronomical foreign debt, now over US$120 billion, despite the US$80 billion paid out in the 1980s). The model was completed by concentrating income in the hands of a wealthy consumer class able to afford the products of the industrialisation process.

The model became known as Brazil's 'economic miracle' and was much admired by many Western economists, yet it left a huge legacy of deprivation and violence. The military treated Brazil's people merely as a factor in an economic equation, using brutal repression and censorship to silence those who tried to protest. Congress was reduced to a rubber stamp body; trade unions, student unions and popular movements were banned and activists persecuted, tortured and killed. The authorities closed down publications and radio stations and censored those that remained.

The military regime ended in 1985, leaving behind both a vast foreign debt and a 'social debt', caused by years of neglect of housing, health, education and sanitation. During its 21 years, for example, the National Housing Bank made 92 per cent of its loans to middle and upper-class housing, almost ignoring the low-income projects it was in principle established to finance.

The civilian governments that followed promised change. President José Sarney announced 'Tudo Pelo Social' (Everything for Social Needs) and his successor, President Fernando Collor, promised priority for the descamisados, the shirtless ones. Instead, corruption, mismanagement and inflation have eaten up government funds and from 1990 a rigid austerity programme has brought recession and severe cuts in public spending.

Consequently, Brazil's children are worse off than they have ever been. In São Paulo a government survey found that 70 per cent of children under 16 are working to help supplement the family income. 'The bad distribution of income is the origin of all the other problems of families and young people', explained a government sociologist.

Despising the future

In 1991 the Brazilian government is waiving US$7.4 billion in tax revenue due from companies with projects in the North and Northeast. Described as 'fiscal incentives', these generous tax holidays are in reality 'a diversion of public money for the illicit personal enrichment of the beneficiary', in the words of one Inland Revenue official. In waiving the taxes, the government is bowing to pressure from politicians in the North and Northeast to renege on its promise to eliminate the incentives.

The sum involved in this one tax break far exceeds the entire 1990 federal budget for education, US$4.7 billion. Of this, over 77 per cent went on higher education, most of it to free federal universities where most of the students come from high income families. Meanwhile four million of Brazil's 31 million school-age children have never been to school. Of the 27 million who go, usually studying in overcrowded, dilapidated buildings for no more than three or four hours a day, 15 million drop out before the end of the fourth year. Only five million finish the full eight years of first grade and, of these, just three million complete their secondary school education. In 1967, 7.4 per cent of the children who began school went on to higher education. In 1989 the proportion had fallen to only 5.9 per cent.

Most of Brazil's street children have had little or no contact with school. Once they are on the street it becomes almost impossible for them to fit into the conventional school system. Although basic education is universally recognised as an essential step towards reducing income concentration and achieving a fairer society 'ten years after the end of the authoritarian regime the Brazilian elites have not taken one step towards social reforms', including a really free national education system, says Cristovam Buarque, rector of the University of Brasília, in his book *The Collapse of Brazilian Modernity* (*O Colapso da Modernidade Brasileira*, Editora Paz e Terra, 1991).

If Brazil chose to make basic education and the elimination of adult illiteracy a priority, it has advantages that most other developing countries would envy. It is the only large third world country which speaks a single language (Portuguese); it has efficient building and publishing industries, human resources, capital and administrative organisation. It has electricity for night classes and a telecommunications system that reaches over 80 per cent of the population. It is the home of an internationally recognised educationalist, Paulo Freire. According to Buarque, the existence of chronic illiteracy in a country with such potential 'is the result of a deliberate option, the decision of the government with the connivance of the elites to use public money for other ends.'

Buarque believes that Brazil's elite needs to be re-educated. The concessions for Brazil's radio and TV channels, which have to be authorised by congress, are not conditional on any form of public service or education. Apart from a few anaemic state TV stations, they are all in private hands. The most influential and commercially successful network is TV Globo, a worldwide exporter of soaps and regular international award-winner. TV Globo offers children the same programme six days a week, five hours a day; a variety show presented by a young woman, Xuxa, in which hundreds of children provide an anonymous, inert background. Its educational and cultural content is zero.

The failure to see education as a national priority has robbed teachers of any prestige — in some states they earn so little that only those who live at home can afford to teach. In Brazil's poorest state, Piaui, children were left for eight months in 1990 without classes while teachers went on strike for a living wage. The governor who denied them a rise spent millions on installing an aquatic park with artificial waves in the capital Teresina and on the eve of his departure from office used public money to buy several thousand dollars worth of food and drink for his own consumption. With such low salaries it was no surprise when an inspection revealed that many lay teachers in Piaui could not even find Brazil on the map. In São Paulo, the wealthiest state, many teachers have to give classes in two or even three schools to make ends meet.

In only one state, Rio de Janeiro, has education been made a priority. During his term in office in the early 1980s, Governor Leonel Brizola built 150 special 'integrated' schools, known as *Centros Integrados de Educaçao Popular* Integrated Centres for Popular Education (CIEPS). Re-elected in 1990, he plans to build 500 more schools. The CIEPS offer a full school day with three meals, a shower, a library and a sports hall. Although they have been labelled political propaganda because of their distinctive facades and have also been criticised as unnecessarily expensive, a visit to Rio's shanty towns shows how important they have become to the poorer population. The CIEPS' elegant buildings rise like magic out of the usual morass of rubbish dumps and shanties, symbolising hope and the promise of escape from misery. One resident described the first days of the local CIEP: 'the children ate every scrap of food on their plates, then invaded the kitchens and scraped clean the pots and pans. They were so unused to having regular meals that they could not understand that next day there would also be food, and the day after, and every day.'

The Federal government has now taken up the idea of the Rio CIEPS and plans to build 5,000 such schools up and down the country. Until that happens the basic schooling administered by state and municipal authorities continues to be far from free. School uniform is compulsory and at the beginning of every school year each family receives a list of material it must supply — books, textbooks, notebooks, glue, coloured pencils, crayons, paper. For families with many children it is an impossible burden. For 1991 the Ministry of Education promised 67 million free books, but three months into the school term they had still not been delivered.

For millions of families school means above all free school meals. They might be the only regular food the children get. Another paradox in a land that is one of the world's top food exporters. Once again for Cristovam Buarque this hunger in a land of plenty is not accidental but 'the result of economic options ... Brazilian hunger is fabricated. It is induced by policies and laws. Since the beginning of colonization, land, techniques and farm labour have been concentrated to generate wealth in international markets' and not to feed the population. With the low level of wages paid in Brazil, local demand for food crops can never compete with the lure of lucrative overseas markets for exports such as soybeans, coffee and orange juice. 'For many decades it will still be more efficient and economic to produce feed for European cattle than for the country's children,' concludes Buarque.

The solution involves changing the property structure and the use of land. 'Brazil has an enormous area of land without people to cultivate it because the owners prefer to leave it unproductive. At the same time there is an enormous number of people without land,' says Buarque. With the need for food that exists in Brazil, unproductive land is irrational and archaic but strongly defended by those who claim to support modernisation.

The result of this land and food policy is that 31 per cent of Brazilian children under five years old suffer from stunted growth. Even the conservative newspaper *O Estado de São Paulo*, commenting on Brazil's shameful record on infant mortality and malnutrition, asked 'Could there be a more efficient formula for despising the future than that adopted by Brazil in the treatment of its children?'

Government initiatives

President Fernando Collor, who took office in March 1990, has adopted a far more sophisticated attitude than his predecessors towards foreign critics of the Brazilian government. In the past, such critics were accused of interference in Brazil's internal affairs, while domestic opponents were condemned as lackeys of imperial interests or foreign bankers who were intent on demoralising the country. In contrast, President Collor has employed the same tactics as he has used to defuse environmental issues — he identifies with the critics, puts himself forward as a champion of their cause, and announces a series of flamboyant measures to tackle the effects while steering well clear of dealing with the causes. On street children, the government's measures have been designed to stop what it calls the 'phenomenon of extermination', but this is treated in isolation from its social, economic and political roots.

In this way, the government never acknowledges responsibility for the millions of rejected children who roam Brazil's streets, and takes no measures to prevent yet more children taking to the streets. On the contrary, in President Collor's first year of government the number of unemployed has risen from 2.5 million to six million and the minimum wage has sunk to its lowest level ever in terms of purchasing power; no more than US$50 to US$60 a month.

Through this new brand of gesture politics, Brazil now has some of the most advanced legislation in the world on child rights. It is one of the few countries to have a Ministry of the Child and has announced a National Plan for the Prevention and Reduction of Violence Against Children. Yet at the same time, its economic and social policies are impoverishing the population and increasing the number of potential child victims. The first ever Children's Minister, Alceny Guerra, appointed to the newly-created post on 30 May 1990, acknowledges that the poverty of large segments of the population 'worsened in recent years by a crisis scenario and stagnation of the economic growth process', has aggravated the situation of violence in Brazil.

In his speech to the World Summit on Children at the United Nations in New York in September 1990, President Collor said he was turning the Council for the Defence of Human Rights attached to the Ministry of Justice into an 'instrument of permanent protection of the physical integrity of Brazilian children ... the Federal Government is already taking measures to see to it that these shameful abuses against children are brought to a halt.'

The new Ministry of the Child has been at pains to stress the measures taken by the government. Brazil has ratified the International Convention on the Rights of the Child, the new Child and Adolescent Statute was passed by Congress and sanctioned by the President, and the national children's agency, FUNABEM, with its much-hated state juvenile remand institutes, the FEBEMs, was replaced by a new agency, the *Fundação Centro Brasileiro para a Infância e Adolescência*, the Central Brazilian Foundation for Infancy and Adolescence (CBIA).

In December 1990 the Minister of Justice set up a national commission containing equal numbers of representatives from government departments and non-governmental organisations dedicated to the defence of children's rights. The commission was to 'elaborate an action proposal aimed at launching a frontal attack on the problem of violence and the extermination of children'. The commission drew up recommendations and then became a permanent working group. The recommendations included:

● investigations of death squad killings by specially picked civil police accompanied by special prosecutors with, if necessary, help from the federal police.

● a review of police human resources policies with new criteria for the recruitment, selection, training and permanent retraining of members of the police force.

● legal sanctions against police officers accused of using violence against children and adolescents.

● restrictions on the participation of police officers in 'parallel activities' and greater control of security companies, especially those employing police officers and security guards who are shown to be members of death squads.

The major flaw in these recommendations, which follow lines suggested by Amnesty International in its report on child killings in Brazil is that police forces are controlled by the states, not the federal government. Each state has both a civilian and military police force. The federal government can only recommend changes, which each state government is then free either to implement or ignore.

Despite the promises, the killing goes on. The death toll for 1990 was higher than ever, and the murders have continued in 1991:

● According to investigations by the president of the bar association in Sergipe state (Northeast Brazil), in 1990 140 under-18s were murdered in the state. Three boys aged 17,16 and 13 who accused policemen of being involved with death squads were sent to another state for safety (*Folha de São Paulo*, 9.1.91).

● In the last six months of 1990, 67 children and adolescents were killed in Salvador, while in Alagoas, another Northeast state, two boys were killed on 26 October 1990 and 29 under-18s, including eight girls, are on a death list prepared by local death squads. Alagoas is President Collor's home state. 'Because of the summer season (December-February) and the consequent arrival of tourists, boys and girls are being persecuted.' said the National Movement of Street Children in a letter sent last year (*Jornal do Brasil*, 18.2.91).

● In Vitória, capital of Espírito Santo state, the Mayor, Vitor Buaiz, deplored the first murders in February 1991. He blamed an organisation called *Organizaçao Pena de Morte*, the Death Penalty Organisation (OPM), 'a group of ex-policemen and serving policemen who last year killed 100 ex-prisoners'. By 13 March eight children and adolescents had been killed (*Jornal do Brasil*, 13.3.91).

A survey carried out jointly by the independent research organisation IBASE and the National Movement of Street Children counted 457 murders of children and adolescents in the three cities of Recife, Rio and São Paulo between March and August 1990. Thirty-eight per cent of those killed lived with their families and only a small proportion had any involvement with crime or drugs. In only 74 cases out of 457 was the murderer identified. They were 'generally policemen or ex-policemen'. Preliminary figures for the first three months of 1991 indicate that nearly 300 young people were murdered in 11 major cities.

NGOs and other initiatives

The best known non-governmental organisation working with children is the National Movement of Street Children, set up in 1985 to fight for the citizenship rights of children and adolescents. The Movement began by condemning police violence and giving children a chance to tell their own stories at a series of national meetings. As a result, enquiries were set up in a number of states and some policemen were expelled from their forces, but in general police impunity remained intact. The Movement has made hundreds of complaints to the authorities, prepared dossiers on crimes, and is represented on the commission set up by the Minister of Justice. Members of the Movement have received death threats, notably its Rio coordinator, Volmer do Nascimento.

Many individuals and organisations, Brazilian and foreign, have been working for years with street children: running shelters, training educators to be on the streets with them, setting up schools, homes, training courses, offering friendship, hope and escape. UNICEF has had an important role in sponsoring projects with educators, while Churches of various denominations, especially the Catholic Church's *Pastoral do Menor* (Children's Pastoral Service), have also been active. Yet it was only the international response to the crescendo of condemnation about the killings by the National Movement of Street Children that jolted the authorities out of their indifference. Amnesty International's 1990 report, followed by TV documentaries shown all over the world, added to the pressure.

The result has been a flurry of activity: the Ministry of the Child; committees and commissions at federal level; parliamentary committees of inquiry in the national congress and the Rio legislative assembly; unprecedented media coverage for books like Gilberto Dimenstein's, and projects with street children. New projects have been set up involving hotels in Rio, carnival samba schools, toy manufacturers, multinational companies and local authorities.

These are all good signs, but the indignation that should be caused by the killing, rejection or abandonment of any child is still lacking. Action is being taken because the world has thrown up its hands in horror, not because that horror is shared by the authorities, the congressmen, the judiciary, or the general public. Furthermore, the reasons behind the existence of so many street children are still only timidly discussed.

The non-governmental organisations can only scratch the surface of such a huge problem — millions of children, and their numbers are growing every year. The federal government might be saying all the correct things about the slaughter but the authorities the children come up against in their day-to-day struggle for survival are the police, and there has so far been little change in their attitude.

In May 1991, over a year after Gilberto Dimenstein's book was first published in Portuguese, the Children's Pastoral Service accused policemen or men dressed in police uniforms of systematic attacks on adolescents living in São Paulo's Cathedral Square, Praça da Sé. Boys had been shot and wounded, burnt with acid, chased and arrested. A 16-year-old pregnant girl had been beaten and policemen had forced girls to strip. All the incidents reported happened in April and May. São Paulo's police chief, Pedro Franco de Campos, replied that the increased police presence in the square had improved safety for pedestrians.

Jan Rocha, May 1991

1

'My life is like the wind'

It is a simple, old, two-storeyed house painted yellow. The windows are protected by grilles and there is a patio at the front. There are no trees and no garden. Inside, there is no furniture and no household electrical appliances, only a table and formica chair. Visitors sit on the floor in one of the less sweltering rooms. The fridge is broken and there is no money to fix it. Despite the heat, which is often over 100 degrees fahrenheit, there is no fan. The place is clean, though it is impossible to stop the dust getting in. However, if you look out across the neighbourhood you realise you are in a comparatively imposing building. The view takes in a kilometre long pile of shacks separated by filthy roads; pregnant women carrying basins full of clothes; ragamuffin children playing with wooden sticks and chunks of metal, improvising games in pools of stagnant water.

The building houses the Catholic Church's *Pastoral do Menor*, the Pastoral Service for Children, in the diocese of Duque de Caxias on the periphery of Greater Rio de Janeiro, one of the most violent regions in Brazil, and inhabited by 3.5 million people. The Pastoral is situated in the Lixão (Big Tip) shanty town where rival gangs battle for control of the drug trade, and the inhabitants scrape a living from petty crime, odd jobs and badly-paid employment. The house is respected by the neighbours as though it was some kind of a temple. During the day the children in their filthy shorts play in the house's narrow corridors. Many of them may end up with their names inscribed in red letters on the rustic two-metre plaque with a white background, strategically placed in the entrance hall. It is the list of children murdered by the death squads of Duque de Caxias.

RELAÇÃO DOS MENINOS(AS) ASSASSINADOS EM DUQUE DE CAXIAS NO PERÍODO DE JANEIRO DE 87 A SETEMBRO DE 88, SEGUNDO A LISTA DA SECRETARIA DA POLÍCIA CIVIL.

DATA (INFORMAÇÕES TEL. 771 88 25)

DATA		IDADE
06.01.87	MICHEL DE SOUZA	6 ANOS
15.01.87	MARCO ANTONIO C. DE FARIAS	15 ANOS
28.01.87	RENATA G. MELLO	2 ANOS
02.02.87	VALBER DE SOUZA	11 ANOS
02.02.87	MARCOS A. DIAS DA SILVA	5 "
04.02.87	SANDRO ALEXANDRE F.	17 "
04.02.87	GILMAR CORDEIRO	17 "
06.02.87	PAULO SERGIO F. DA S.	11 "
08.02.87	DAVI GREGORIO	
11.02.87	TIBÉRIO C. SANTOS	
13.02.87	REGINALDO BRAZ B.	
19.02.87	ALOIZIO M. ACIOL	
21.02.87	MARCOS AURELIO	
23.02.87	ALEXANDRE BRA	
24.02.87	CARLOS JOSÉ DE	
24.02.87	ANTONIO F. DOS SA	
26.02.87	FÁBIO JOSÉ DA S	
06.03.87	AGRINALDO F.	
07.03.87	JURANDIS	
08.03.87		
21.03.8		
23.03		
30.03		
05.0		
09		
11.		
18.04		
19.04.		
21.04.8		
04.8		

DATA		IDADE
05.8.87	EDNALDO N. DA SILVA	
14.08.87	DARIO LOPES	16 ANOS
27.08.87	FABIANO V. NEIRA	14 ANOS
30.08.87	CARLOS ALBERTO M.S.	17 "
30.08.87	ISMAEL SERGIO D.	16 "
01.09.87	ISAIAS DO NASCIMENTO	17 "
10.09.87	RECEM-NATO	15 "
12.09.87	MANOEL LIMA S.	17 ANOS
.9.87	MARCOS DA SILVA N.	16 "
.87	DOUGLAS RIBEIRO SILVA	3 "
.87	FÁBIO CARLOS DE A.	17 "
.87	CHARLES DE OLIVEIRA	16
.87	VIVIANE C. NOBREGA DA SILVA	4
.87	ANTONIO C. ROSA VIEIRA	17
.87	JORGE LÚCIO A. MELLO	17
0.87	JOVANE JERÔNIMO	
16.10.87	EDUARDO GOMES DOS S.	
02.11.87	MARCOS A. DA SILVA	
05.11.87	ROBSON A. FORTES	
03.12.87	MARCIO ROBERTO OLIVEIRA	
.12.87	EDSON RODRIGUES DA S.	
	PAULO VINICIUS R. SOUZA	
	...XANDRE	
	...RTO DE CARVALHO	
	...A. DOS SANTOS	
	...OS (CATITA)	
	...O ANTUNES	
	...G. DIAS	
	...M. DE OL	
	...S. GONÇ	

These days the list is not quite so carefully maintained. 'I have stopped counting. It wore me down. I found that each time we protested at the death of a child, more children were killed. It seemed like they were taking their revenge', says Volmer do Nascimento, 38, worker at the *Fundaçao Nacional de Bem-Estar do Menor*, the National Foundation for Child Welfare (FUNABEM), ex-leader of the Children's Pastoral Service and currently one of the coordinators of the *Movimento Nacional de Meninos e Meninas de Rua*, the National Movement of Street Children. Volmer, who spends part of his time at the Pastoral's house, adds sadly, 'We don't have any money to spare at all. We have just one paid worker and he gets the minimum wage. Even then, we can hardly manage to pay him. But I bet there would be plenty of money available in Brazil or abroad if an academic wanted to write a thesis on the problem of abandoned street children.'

Volmer is delicate and dark-skinned, a fast and physically expressive speaker. For the last four years he has brought the children of the shanty town together to discuss their lives and try and find solutions to their problems. In 1986 he began to realise, that dozens of the children who spent time at the Pastoral house were disappearing. He and his wife, Joana D'Arc, who have two children of their own, began to investigate. They soon discovered that the children were being exterminated by the death squads of Greater Rio de Janeiro with the discreet support of the police.

Supported by the Catholic Church, Volmer alerted the authorities to the systematic murder of children, most of whom were supposedly responsible for petty crimes. This provoked the wrath of the death squads and the police in the region. One day, a well-known killer approached him and, smiling, said, 'Volmer, it's your turn next, isn't it?' Dom Mauro Morelli, Bishop of Duque de Caxias, was also threatened. One of his diocesan workers answered the telephone one day and heard a cavernous voice say, 'Tell that lousy bishop that we have got him in our sights.'

Since Volmer publicly accused people by name, he has received a stream of anonymous threats over the phone. He named, among others, João Pedro Bueno, known as 'Pedro the Devil', and his son João Alberto Neves Bueno, both employed by the Justice Department. Answering the phone on one occasion, he received an even darker threat than usual. A voice said, 'I think the best way to get you to stop is to kill your two children.'

Volmer and his wife refused to give in as they felt that the killers ran too great a political risk if they tried to kill the family. 'I know that one day they will get me. They won't kill me now because I

pointed a finger at a lot of people and they would all be
ects. But the day my work leaves the public eye or if I stop
working with children, I am a dead man', says Volmer.

A silent war

The case of Volmer and the children of Duque de Caxias is not an
isolated one, nor is it the most dramatic. In the backstreets of the
country's big cities, a silent war of extermination is being waged
against young petty criminals. The war involves the use of beatings
and torture. Although the exclusively police death squads of the
1970s have practically ceased to exist, this latest war is promoted
and organised by members of the police force. The groups involved
are often given names such as 'death squads' and *justiceiros*
('avengers'), and the police encourage their activities on the grounds
that the children are dangerous and will never mend their ways.
The police and death squads do not target children for the sake of
it, but because they see them as criminals. Children are increasingly
to be found among their victims because growing numbers are
forced on to the street to make a living, to contribute to the family
income or because there is no school for them.

The war on children is one of the least known aspects of Brazil's
social crisis. According to the Ministry of Labour, unemployment
is three times higher among juveniles than among adults. Official
statistics also show that 44 per cent of children and adolescents are
from families with a per capita income of half the minimum wage,
while half of these families have a per capita income of a quarter
of the minimum wage. There are 27 million children, therefore,
living in a state of poverty which reproduces and cultivates violence,
and provides an ideal climate for the growth of the death squads.

Although it is difficult to be precise, and the tendency is for
underestimation, the number of children murdered by the death
squads for their supposed involvement in petty crime reached an
average of approximately one a day in 1989. Out of every 100
children in the country who are victims of a violent death, 33 are
killed by the death squads. In Rio de Janeiro alone, from January
to July 1989, 184 children and adolescents were murdered.

To get an idea of the scale of these killings, it is enough to
remember that in the Lebanese civil war, when the whole country
was in flames, 850 people were killed in the six months from March
to August 1989. During this period, in Lebanon, according to official

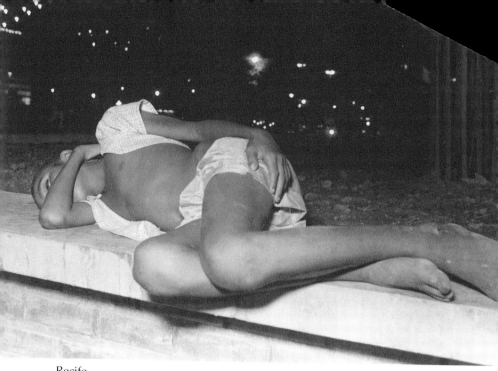

Recife.

statistics and the Red Cross, 30 children died as a result of the war; this figure includes both bomb blast victims and murders.

'There is definitely a process of extermination of young people going on in various parts of the country. And I have to recognise that, unfortunately, there are members of the police force who are involved in the killing or who are giving protection to the killers', admits Hélio Saboya, head of the Justice Department in Rio de Janeiro, and a former human rights activist. 'When I look at the death squads, there are moments when I can't tell who are the crooks and who are the police', adds Almeida Filho, head of the Justice Department in Pernambuco, the biggest state in the country's north-east region. He is accustomed to reading reports of murders of young people in which the victims have suffered the most sadistic torture: genital organs severed, eyes poked out, bodies burned by cigarette ends and slashed by knives.

In Pernambuco, TV Viva, a video production company run by the Luiz Freire Centre, an organisation linked to the human rights movement, made a film about the killing of children by the death squads. They found that, in the first few months of 1988, an average of three children were killed by death squads every week. The video took a year and a half to make. When the film was ready, TV Viva d to include a final sequence noting the murder of some of the children who appeared in the video. Some of the mothers interviewed by TV Viva were able to give the names of police officers who were implicated in the murder of their children, but the producers preferred to edit out this information because some of the police officers mentioned were stationed in the same neighbourhood as the company in Olinda. The police would have inevitably taken revenge if their names had been mentioned in the film. One of the boys, nicknamed Rusty, was already on the police's hit list. He left on film a tragic prophecy of his own fate: 'My life is like the wind. Nothing can stop it blowing away.'

Voices from the street

'We sniff glue because we need to. We steal — watches, necklaces. We don't have anywhere to eat, we don't have anywhere to sleep, we don't have anywhere to stay — that's why we steal. I steal, I walk around, I sniff glue, and then I can't do anything. I haven't got a Dad — he died seven years ago. I have eight brothers and sisters and I can't really stay at home, so I live on the street. That's how I lead my life.

I'd like all of us to be able to work, so we all could be healthy and have a house to live in. We should all have our rights, we should have our hope and our family alive. We shouldn't need this death squad to kill people, we shouldn't need to rob or steal anything.

I started living on the street when I was seven years old, when I lost my mother and couldn't survive. Me and my brother were hungry and then a friend of mine took me to the street. When I got to the Brasagiaria I became a prostitute. Then I started to steal because as a prostitute I couldn't support my family. When I was thieving the men came to arrest me, they beat me up and did a lot of things. They put me in jail where I had to eat bread and water and spent three days in isolation, before I was taken to the FEBEM (Foundation for Child Welfare) and beaten up again. I used to spend one or two months in prison and then I would escape to the street again. I used to take drugs and start stealing again, and then get arrested and beaten up. Always stealing and getting beaten up. When I got fed up with being beaten I went back to being a prostitute, but then the bastards slapped me around if I didn't want to have sex with them. If I was to tell that to the policemen they would just put me in jail and beat me up again.

It hurts to be beaten by other people because they are not our parents and never brought us up. They don't know why we are on the streets and they never even try to find out. They just beat us up because they think we are thieves and bad people. They speak badly of us, but they

A street life: profile of 'Beto'

Name: 'Beto'

Age: 14

Occupation: Used to work crushing cardboard. Now sells sweets and fruit at traffic lights. Walks the streets, runs away from the police and sniffs glue. Sleeps in the street.

Ambitions: Meet the TV compere Silvio Santos. Buy his mother a house at 'Porta da Esperança' [gate of hope].

Heroes: 'I don't really have any....I don't know anyone that good.'

Virtues: Protects the girls in his group.

Faults: Sniffs glue.

Successes: Silence — no reply

Mistakes: 'I didn't want to turn out like this.'

Would like to meet: TV stars in the street. 'Anyone.'

Would like to avoid: The police.

Favourite film: *Rambo* and Stallone *Cobra*.

Favourite book: 'Primary school exercise book.'

Favourite music: *Between kisses and blows* and *Summer dreams* by the country and western duo, Leandro and Leonardo.

Favourite food: 'Anything.'

Hobbies: Watching Mutant Ninja Turtles on the television sets in shop windows.

Philosophy of life: Share with friends. Hit or run away from enemies, depending on their size.

Religion: 'I wanted to be a Catholic, but a Catholic that goes to work. There's no way I would want to be part of one of those evangelical churches.'

Favourite city: 'Well it has to be the one I'm living in, don't you think?'

Source: *Folha de São Paulo*

Adopting the dead

The activities of the Rio de Janeiro death squads have given rise to a bizarre and tragic phenomenon: the adoption of dead children. The child may not even be known by his adoptive parents but will be buried under their name. 'It is a sad irony, a macabre game. A boy who spent his life on his own gets a father only after he's dead', comments Maria Tereza Moura, ex-coordinator of Rio de Janeiro's Street Children Movement.

When a body arrives at the *Instituto Médico Legal*, the Legal Medical Institute (IML), with signs of violence, the death certificate must register the name of the victim before the body can be buried. If no member of the family lays claim to the body, the body cannot be buried. The social welfare organisations have found an imaginative way out of this dilemma. They find parents willing to adopt the child posthumously and give it their family name. In this way, the formalities necessary to get the body out of the IML and to a decent burial are complied with.

The mother of one murder victim in Nova Iguaçu told how she saw her son killed by two members of a death squad well known in the neighbourhood. The killers did not even bother to wear a mask. After killing the boy, they went into the house and warned the weeping mother, 'If you tell the police or any of these church people, we'll kill you and the rest of your family.' She did not go to the police or to the IML to identify the body.

These stories show the obstacles to establishing with precision the number of young people killed by the death squads. The statistics compiled by human rights movements and the National Movement of Street Children undoubtedly underestimate the problem, although they both show the rising tide of violence in the country.

According to the Ministry of Health, violent deaths among the 15-17 age group jumped from 54.3 per cent of all causes of death in 1979 to 65 per cent in 1986. In some of the country's biggest cities, murder is the biggest cause of death among children and adolescents. Other sources support this conclusion. According to a survey by Rio de Janeiro's Justice Department, there were 172 recorded murders of minors in 1985. The number rose to 204 in 1986, 227 in 1987 and 244 in 1988. The survey was done towards the end of 1989 and had already recorded 184 murders between January and July, more than for the whole of 1985.

O Instituto Brasileiro de Análises Sociais e Econômicas (IBASE), a human rights and research organisation directed by the sociologist Herbert (Betinho) de Souza, is the main source of information about the death squads and their bloody but undeclared war. The information provided by IBASE shows that the number of young people being murdered by the death squads is increasing — and fast.

'The statistics are shaky, incomplete', says Rodrigo Souza Filho, coordinator of the IBASE survey. 'This shows that the authorities are not really bothered about the deaths of poor street children and juvenile delinquents. You only have to compare the statistics that are available on AIDS, a disease which is closely monitored by the

Rio.

Ministry of Health. This is because middle-class people might get AIDS, but it is extremely unlikely that a middle-class child will be killed by the death squads', he adds.

Rodrigo works for the National Movement of Street Children, and is one of the people who inspired IBASE's research. His 'office', provided by a charitable organisation in Rio de Janeiro, shows just how few resources the movement has. The room contains an old wooden shelf full of papers, a table and two old dark wooden chairs. There is just enough room for three people to sit down. Anybody else has to stand outside the door. This tiny room contains much valuable information, especially a file on the death of children, but there is not enough money available even to put the material in alphabetical order, let alone computerise it. There is a real risk that the information will be lost.

2

'I killed you because you had no future'

The shanty town of Calabar lies in the heart of a middle-class area of Salvador. It is the home of various gangs of crooks but it also has a history of community organisation, a process led by the journalist Fernando Conceição. The community wanted to try and stop its young people slipping into street crime, by creating other options to fill the vacuum left by the lack of schooling. The aim was to give the children basic training in a profession or trade, so they set up practical workshops to teach local children how to make bread, ice-cream, soap and so on. The end products were sold and the proceeds shared out between the workshops and the children.

The experiment has been successful, but has had to put up with competition from the local drug gangs who poach the children from the workshops. 'It is unfair competition. They earn five times more working in the drug trade than working in our bakery', complains Fernando Conceição.

There is strong evidence that gangs use children for criminal activities because, in law, minors are not held responsible for their actions. 'Juvenile crime is on the increase, and it's rising fast. Minors are now responsible for most of the robberies committed in Rio de Janeiro', says Liborni Siqueira, of the police children's department in Rio de Janeiro.

Children work for adults who receive stolen goods or as couriers in the drug trade. They are cheap, easily replaceable labour. It is common for the children to become addicted themselves and then run errands in exchange for a gram of cocaine or a pot of glue to sniff. Besides making them high, glue eases their hunger. The addiction further reduces the chance of going to school or getting a job.

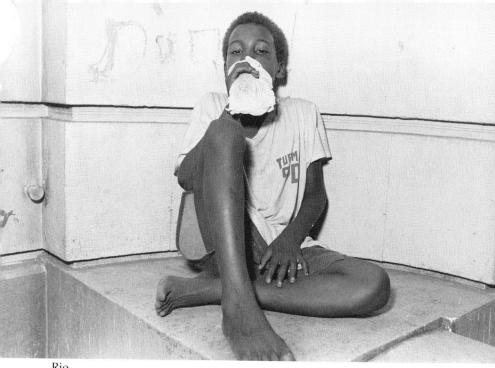

Rio.

When Rio de Janeiro University carried out some research on street children the subject of drugs inevitably came up. The psychologists involved in the research soon realised how difficult it would be to try and convince the children to give up drugs. A drug addict from a middle-class background could at least be offered the prospect of a better life once off drugs. There was little to offer somebody whose destiny is likely to be at best, scratching a living and at worst, a torture session at the local police station and a bullet in the head. When one of the university psychologists asked why the children sniffed glue every day, one replied, 'Well, have you got a better suggestion?'

School's out

One of the few ways of breaking the vicious circle that traps street children is to give them the education they need to find a job, but the educational system refuses to accept responsibility for their schooling, especially if they have been 'in trouble'. Most of the children are undisciplined and aggressive, and many lack even the documents needed to enable them to register at a school. Nor do they have anybody who could take them along to register. If they manage to get past this stage, they are faced with a curriculum which seems irrelevant to their lives.

Yet there are also examples of how money, time and patience can overcome these obstacles. The São Geraldo Institute, managed by a Jesuit, Clovis Piazza, looks after a number of children who have been involved in petty crime. Clovis is an Italian, who in his own country worked in the church's prison pastoral service. He studied economics, philosophy and psychology, and uses his knowledge of psychology to try and understand the aggressive attitude of the children in his care. His attempts to gain the confidence of the children can take years, and do not always succeed. If he manages to gain the confidence of one of the children, there is another bridge to be crossed. 'The child begins to think of you as his father, as protection. Unconsciously, he begins to provoke you. He treats you as if you were the person who abandoned him in the street, as if it was you who had thrust him into this world of violence. If you don't understand this phase, if you react by rejecting the child, then all is lost', explains Piazza.

The education system is unable even to carry out its basic functions. There has been an increase in absenteeism from school and the general level of education provided is poor. Only 13 per cent of children who enter primary school stay the course. This kind of statistic makes it difficult to imagine that the system will be able to produce many people like Piazza whose training in psychology gives him an understanding of how children think and whose background in the church has taught him the virtues of solidarity.

The end result is that children who enter the world of petty crime are fed a diet of violence and are excluded from any possibility of finding honest work. Crime becomes the only way of keeping themselves alive and aggression becomes the normal pattern of behaviour. 'Violence is like a game of ping-pong. If you hit the ball hard, it comes back at you just as hard', says Father Piazza.

These circumstances produce highly dangerous young people who will kill in cold blood and for whom any therapeutic treatment becomes practically useless. According to psychologists who have juvenile delinquents in their care, most of them come from homes where they were regularly beaten by their mother or father, and beaten hard. Living rough is not much different. The children who live or work on the street have endless stories of beatings inflicted by the police in the early morning hours when the rest of the city is sleeping. Children are often tortured even in official correction centres.

The Franciscan priest Márcio Arruda Terra is accustomed to violence against children, and to the silence that shrouds the situation. He is the parish priest of Our Lady of Fátima church at the top of Cantagalo Hill in Ipanema, one of the most celebrated and sophisticated neighbourhoods of Rio de Janeiro. Known as 'comrade' by the boys and other residents of the hillside, he is short and thin, with thick-rimmed spectacles. He likes to dress in sandals, a t-shirt and bermuda shorts. Father Márcio has a good neighbours policy with the local gangs, such as the 'Medellín Army', which control the drug trade in Ipanema. There, as in other neighbourhoods, violence is not committed only by the police, but is often the result of wars between rival gangs.

One of Father Márcio's boys, Patrício Hilário da Silva, was nine years old. He went to church every day, where he liked to watch the priest's video films. On 1 May, he failed to appear, and his body was found on the beach soon afterwards. He had been strangled and a note left on his body, 'I killed you because you didn't go to school and had no future.'

Father Márcio recalls last New Year's Eve, when some children came to his house to celebrate and watch the traditional fireworks on the shore. There is a magnificent view from the church grounds.

Padre Márcio Terra, Rio.

When the firework display began, the youngest of the children refused to leave the house to watch them. 'Come and see how beautiful it looks. There are all kinds of pretty and coloured fireworks', said Father Márcio. 'I am scared of getting shot', replied the boy, who was convinced that the noise was really a shoot-out, a common event in the area. 'Violence is such a routine thing for them', explains Márcio.

One case in particular shocked the priest. In October 1989, a policeman beat up a boy known as 'Macarrão' who used to go to Márcio's church. The policeman hit him for ten minutes until he was lying bleeding on the floor. There were several witnesses but nobody did anything, and after beating the boy up, the policeman went over to a nearby bar, sat down and calmly drank a glass of beer. Only when the police had disappeared did Macarrão's friends carry him off and look for medical help. 'Don't you want me to tell the Brazilian Lawyers' Order?', Márcio asked the boy. 'No', came the reply. 'This time they beat me up, next time, they'll kill me.'

One sunny day in 1989, Sisters Beatriz and Ivanir decided to make a photograph album of the boys who attended the centre for abandoned children in Vila Gláucea on the outskirts of Nova Iguaçu, Greater Rio de Janeiro. The centre is maintained by the main school in Duque de Caxias, the Saint Anthony College. The Sisters only wanted a memento of the children. They bought some films and, camera in hand, tried to round them up, but the boys refused point blank to be photographed. The Sisters understood and did not insist. The boys feared that the album might fall into the hands of the police or the death squads. They could be recognised and hunted down.

We received the same reaction at first when we asked for photographs for this book. One of them said, 'The album will end up in the hands of the men.' The children only agreed to be photographed by Paula Simas after negotiations with intermediaries who they trusted like Volmer do Nascimento, Sister Ivanir, in charge of the centre, and Tiana Sá, Rio's state coordinator of the Movement of Street Children. Even then, they insisted on covering their faces. One of them, a boy whom others had sworn to kill, allowed Sister Ivanir to hide his features with her hand. 'These boys are scared to death', says Sister Ivanir. 'And they have good reason to be.'

The centre and its workshops are situated on a small slope. The garden is carefully tended by the boys, and the trees are full of fruit. It is quiet and the air is pure, bearing little resemblance to most Rio de Janeiro shanty towns. Sister Ivanir likes to go round wearing light summer clothes and a beret on her head. She loves climbing trees

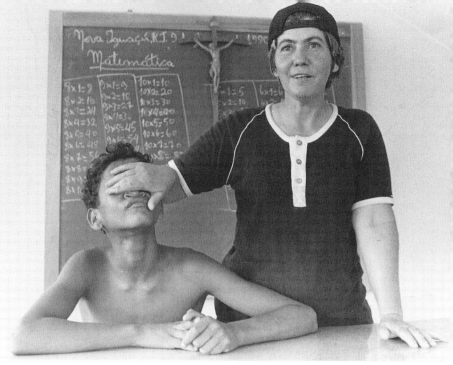

Sister Ivanir, Rio.

to pick fruit or to untangle a stray kite. But her calm disappears when she, the boys, or the assistant, Sebastião Couto, start to talk about the violence.

The centre owes its existence to the widespread violence. It was established in response to the murder and torture of boys in Duque de Caxias. It feeds those who have nowhere to eat and provides a haven for anyone on the run from the police or the death squads. 'I know they will kill me if I go back to Caxias', says one of the boys. The immense majority of them arrive at the centre with marks and bruises on their bodies. 'Some of them have been beaten up so badly they arrive in a terrible state. Others come here thoroughly depressed and just looking for a quiet corner where they can go to sleep', says Sister Ivanir.

The inauguration of the centre caused a commotion in the neighbourhood. The local residents passed round a petition against it, accusing Sister Ivanir of being mad and the 'godparent of crooks'. A man suspected of belonging to one of the death squads came up to Sebastião Couto and said, 'Sebastião, these boys have no future. You are wasting your time. They're not worth it.'

If there is a robbery in the neighbourhood, Sister Ivanir's boys always get the blame and the residents of Vila Gláucea step up their protests. In order to avoid greater friction with the neighbours, Sister Ivanir has established strict rules. Firstly, no glue-sniffing is allowed. 'The rule is obeyed. And just imagine, they work with shoemaker's glue in the leather workshops. They never sniff it', she enthuses. 'They are not allowed to take stolen property into the house, and above all, we tell them not to steal anything in the neighbourhood. It is a kind of code of honour, and if anyone breaks it, they are not allowed back. But they obey it. The place is well respected because it is welcoming. They don't get hit and they are given something to eat', continues Sister Ivanir. One boy, the head of a gang, promised her, 'Look aunty, don't worry because we shan't touch this area.'

Although she may be in charge at the centre, there is nothing she can do about what goes on outside. Many of the boys leave never to return. She sometimes discovers that they were murdered by the death squads or in gang fights.

Heavy treatment

Márcia da Silva Valadão, now 16, lived on Largo de Carioca street in Rio de Janeiro for three years. She used to sell sweets there. 'I

Márcia da Silva Valadão.

The feeling of insecurity among the general population creates a perfect environment for the growth of groups claiming to dispense justice. They set about the task of killing 'juvenile delinquents', soon gaining power and respect and building up contacts with the police and even political organisations. They give themselves the pompous name of *justiceiros*, self appointed executors of 'justice'. They enjoy the protection of the police, who believe that the death squads are helping them do their job by removing criminals from the street. Supporting the death squads also wins votes. In his successful campaign for state representative in São Paulo, Erasmo Dias, former head of the Justice Department, put forward a stark proposal for dealing with the prison population. 'We should create concentration camps', he said.

Some death squads were formed for non-financial motives but, with time, became lucrative businesses. The first, and most violent group in São Bernardo was created for vengeance. In 1986, a shopkeeper was murdered and his brothers decided to kill the murderer. After this, their first operation, they went on to carry out similar attacks against criminals or supposed criminals, recruiting willing neighbours skilled with weapons. Soon, the *justiceiros* came under the sway of a youth known as Silvinho, noted for his daring and the nonchalance with which he killed in cold blood. Eventually Silvinho's excesses forced the police to go after him, and he had to flee.

Silvinho would talk with great pride about his work. He liked to walk down the street wearing a hat in the style of 'Indiana Jones', his gun ostentatiously tucked into his belt. One of his trade marks was to shoot his victims five times in the head. Maybe it was superstition, for he certainly believed in extra-terrestrial forces. It was said that he could not be harmed because his grandfather had carved a seven-pointed star on the handle of his .38 calibre gun. The star was a symbol from 'macumba', the African-inspired religion. He had one other protection: he was only 17 years old and, in law, was not legally responsible for his actions.

One of Silvinho's group was arrested after murdering a PT activist. José Martines dos Santos, nicknamed Canarinho (Little Canary), killed the woodworker Joíldes Alvarenga Valadão in the middle of a meeting of the Workers Party in the Pai Heroí shanty town, São Bernardo. 'He had been provoking me for a long time', claimed Canarinho. 'He was always staring at my woman. When they told me that he had been upsetting her again, I decided that I was going to end it once and for all.' He went straight to the meeting and in front of 50 people fired five shots at Joíldes. In prison,

Canarinho told a journalist from the *Jornal do Brasil* that he had come to São Paulo in search of a job. He needed the money to undergo medical treatment. 'I was very tense. I was always wanting to hit everybody at home. I couldn't go very long without hitting out at someone', he said.

The death squads recruit many youngsters like Silvinho to frustrate the legal system. It is a good deal for the youngsters, who earn some money and, above all, acquire great prestige in the neighbourhood. In one anti-death-squad operation in 1988, 'Gilberto', a 16 year old known as Coquinho (Little Rooster), was arrested. He recounted how he joined the death squads, 'Somebody who used to rob people in our neighbourhood mugged me and stole all my money. He was the first person I ever killed.' He calmly told the official questioning him that he had killed seven people in his career as a member of the death squads. Coquinho felt that he had been arrested unjustly. 'I have only killed people who were good for nothing', he said.

The victims

The statements in the dossier put together by the Children's Pastoral Service in Duque de Caxias show that juveniles are accustomed to the presence of hired killers in their neighbourhood. Statement no. 1, from a 14-year-old boy, is particularly illustrative. For the purposes of this book, we have edited down the repetitive and broken sentences of the original statement. We should emphasise that the children often do not differentiate between the police and the unofficial death squads, describing them all simply as 'the police'.

'Let me tell you about a friend of mine who got killed. He was shot in the street. He didn't even have time to draw breath. By the time we got to him, he was already dead. We don't do anything to harm them, we don't swear at them or anything. We nick things from the bar because we are hungry. Then this so-called 'White Hand' appears, killing whoever he feels like. He should give us a chance. All my friends are getting killed.'

Statement no. 5 is from a witness, aged 31. 'Once I saw a boy killed while he was sitting on a shoe-shiner's box. A police car came by almost immediately afterwards. The killer took out his identity card and showed it to the police. He obviously had protection. He went back to check that the boy was dead and then, with the police looking on, he ran off.'

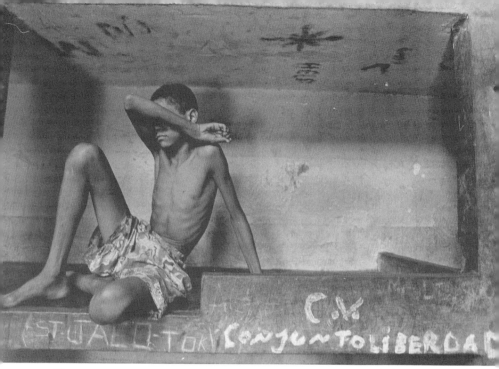

Rio.

These are just a few examples of death-squad murders in Rio de Janeiro. They no longer shock the population, but the people who work with the street children often find their deaths hard to take, especially if, after years of care, the child has shown signs of being able to find a place for himself in society. One such case was that of Gilberto Girão, nicknamed Beto.

Beto, 16, had been living on the streets of Rio since he was four years old. His mother used to sell peanuts at a bus stop near Duque de Caxias Shopping Centre. Beto learned all the tricks of street life and soon became leader of the boys who used to hang round the Praça do Pacificador. He had first option on all the girls in the area, and the others could only court the girls with Beto's permission. He was respected by the other street children, but often harassed and arrested by the police. He complemented his earnings from odd jobs with the proceeds of petty crime.

Beto began to call in at the Pastoral centre. The first sign of a change came when he asked the people there to teach him how to write. He made one request. He wanted one-to-one tuition because he feared it would spoil his image as leader if it got out that he was illiterate. With pencil and paper in hand, Beto made a great effort to learn, and as time went by, he began to acquire other interests.

He was given a shoe-shiner's fixed chair, much more up-market than the portable boxes that the street children usually carry around on their backs.

Beto's progress came to a halt at the beginning of April 1988, when he was arrested and taken to Police Station 59 in Duque de Caxias. The station head was Henrique Alves Pinheiro, who has branded Dom Mauro Morelli an idiot, accused priests of being communists and denied the existence of secret graveyards. Beto's girlfriend and mother claimed he was being beaten up at the station. The Children's Pastoral Service demanded that Beto be released because the law says that a minor cannot be detained in the same place as adults, but Pinheiro refused to let him go. He said that Beto was not a minor, but a 'highly dangerous criminal', and insisted that the Pastoral workers leave his office claiming, say the workers, that they intended to try and help the boy escape. 'I'm not wasting my time talking to people who come here to defend criminals', he said.

The Pastoral workers then went to criminal court office 5 and showed Beto's identity card to the officials there. One of the officials accompanied them back to the Police Station with a warrant ordering the police chief to send the boy on to FUNABEM. 'You got him out of prison, but you haven't saved his life', said the irritated police chief. 'He is being hunted in Duque de Caxias. If he comes back, I doubt if he will survive a single week.' His forecast proved correct. Beto fled from FUNABEM and on 4 September his bullet-ridden body was found under a viaduct. To this day, no one has identified his murderer.

Beto's death bore the hallmarks of a death-squad operation. Before executing their victims, they torture them to make an example of them. In Pernambuco, the death-squad trademarks are particularly grotesque. They burn their victims, poke their eyes out, castrate them and slash their bodies with knives. The Pernambuco death squads also use a .12 calibre shotgun to disfigure the faces of their victims using fewer bullets. 'Some of the torture practised in Pernambuco makes the German SS activities look innocuous', says Rafael Indlenkofer, a German who works with street children in Recife.

One victim of the Pernambuco death squads was Marcos Alexandre da Silva, 17. Marcos lived on the streets with his girlfriend and their baby son. He was often harassed by the police and on at least one occasion, he fought back. According to statements from eye witnesses, collected by *SOS Criança* (SOS Children), he got into a fight with policemen on Monday, 12

December 1988. The police provoked the argument by confiscating Marcos' watch, claiming it was stolen property.

The following day Marcos was leaning against a car, babe in arms, while his wife was out looking for food. Policemen came up, kicked him and told him to clean up the area. Marcos refused and the police hit him with their batons. Passers-by tried to intervene, but Marcos put the baby down and hit back at the police. Later on that day, he was harassed several times by the police. The next day he was grabbed by the police, handcuffed and beaten so badly that blood poured from his mouth and he screamed with pain. The police told his girlfriend that Marcos had stolen a watch.

The women of SOS Children were alerted and went off to try and find Marcos. They learned that he had been arrested and that the police had forged his age so they could hold him in the same police station as adults. Marcos was released but, like Beto in Duque de Caxias, freedom did not mean safety. On 2 February 1989 his disfigured body was found along with that of another woman (not the mother of his child) at the side of a road. He was tied to a tree and almost unrecognisable. His body was full of bullet holes, some of them from a .12 calibre shotgun. The woman had been slashed with knives, burned and shot many times. The murders were attributed to the death squads. Witnesses saw Marcos being kidnapped by men in a white Volkswagen including someone they identified as the plain clothes policeman Anderson Leite Xavier, usually known as 'Alan'.

4

Heroes or villains?

Six months after the death of Marcos Alexandre da Silva, there was another murder in the same style. This time, the victim was Pedro Rodrigues. The crime would normally have gone unnoticed, but things had changed since Marcos' death. Pernambuco's Governor Arraes had created a special squad of officers in the Homicide Division which was digging away trying to unearth evidence about death-squad activities. In addition, two days before his murder, Pedro Rodrigues had made a statement to the police accusing Maria José Borges, 46, of being a drug dealer. The case ended up serving as an example of the links between the death squads and organised crime.

Few people knew Maria José Borges by her real name. She was known as the 'Queen of Coelhos', the most powerful person in the neighbourhood of Coelhos in central Recife. At election time, hordes of candidates would seek her out to ask her help in winning votes. Although she cultivated her image as a community leader by supporting crèches and works of charity, it was an open secret that she was involved in the drug trade. It was also known that she recruited young boys and girls from the neighbourhood to deliver the drugs. She had been accused but never arrested for lack of proof, and her police file had simply disappeared. She had no criminal record.

Nevertheless, she felt threatened when Pedro Rodrigues, a well-known juvenile delinquent, signed a written statement accusing her of being one of the main drug dealers in Recife. Everybody knew this to be true. Maria's response was harsh — Pedro was executed. Whoever talks too much pays the price. Maria mistakenly relied on her traditional impunity, stemming from her friendship with influential politicians and police officers. When she was arrested under suspicion of ordering Pedro's death, she claimed she was the victim of a political plot. 'They want to destroy my political base. Everybody knows I hold the key to thousands of votes in Coelhos', she said.

Inspector Magno Nunes da Costa of the Homicide squad and Almeida Filho, head of the Justice Department Secretariat, received information that the Queen of Coelhos' friends intended to organise her escape and they redoubled security at Bom Pastor, the Women's Prison where she was being held. They also learned that police officers were secretly organising a petition calling for her release and demanding money from Coelhos shopkeepers to pay her lawyers. The shopkeepers knew the rules of the game and did not hesitate to contribute. They even went to the police station to make statements in support of Borges.

One fact in particular caught Almeida Filho's attention. Twenty-seven officers from the Drug Squad of the local police force had visited Borges in prison to declare their support for her. One of them even got into a fight with the warders because he wanted to continue talking for longer than was allowed by prison regulations.

Inspector Nunes pulled off one coup by managing to get ordinary people in Coelhos to admit they were unhappy with the 'Queen's' control of the neighbourhood. The statements contained the names of police officers in the pay of Borges, many of whom were also suspected of involvement in the death squads. Anderson Leite Xavier ('Alan'), accused of killing Marcos Alexandre, was among those mentioned. It transpired that in addition to being paid by Borges for his work in the drug trade, 'Alan' lived with one of her daughters.

As the investigation proceeded, there was bloodshed, as people who feared exposure organised the murders of informers or suspected informers. Just when the arrest of a police officer or death-squad member was expected, the informer would be found dead. Despite these obstacles, the final report of the investigative team concluded that shopkeepers were buying protection from the death squads. It also showed that the people responsible for murdering criminals or suspected criminals were involved in organised crime, including drug dealing. 'These groups have been acting like criminal gangs', said Inspector Nunes when announcing a series of charges at the end of 1989.

Gustavo Augusto Rodrigues de Lima, the Pernambuco public prosecutor chosen to accompany the investigation led by Inspector Nunes, declared he was convinced that the death squads carry out the murder of criminals for propaganda purposes. The death squads' victims are generally dangerous and well-known criminals guilty of armed robberies or muggings. The murder of such criminals serves as an advertisement for the death squads and covers up other crimes by misleading the local public into believing that the death squads are defending the community.

In São Bernardo in the 1980s, the poor neighbourhoods were dominated by gangs which forced residents to pay protection money to avoid being harassed. This led in turn to the creation of death squads, which were paid by the residents to get rid of the gangs. After cleaning the place up, the death squads threatened shopkeepers and other residents with violence if they didn't go on paying. Some of them even encouraged their relations and friends in the North East to come down to São Paulo and join them in this lucrative new business. The hired killer has always been a familiar part of the landscape in the North East.

Although many death-squad leaders are held in great esteem by large sectors of society for their persecution of 'criminals', the police and the human rights movement are both well aware that the death squads soon turn from combatting crime (as they perceive it) to carrying out a whole range of crimes from drug dealing to armed robbery. 'To think that you can fight crime using death squads is like imagining that you can fight obesity by eating sugar', declares a lawyer, Hélio Bicudo, head of Legal Affairs at the São Paulo city administration.

After the kidnapping (see chapter 6) of Luís Tenderine, President of the Justice and Peace Commission in Recife, the *Movimento pela Vida* (Movement for Life) demanded that Governor Miguel Arraes take action against the death squads. The document circulated by the Movement for Life urged Arraes to try and explain the true nature of the death squads to the public. Below are some sections from this manifesto:

● The death squads are instruments of organised crime. They are responsible for a wide range of criminal actions that are harmful to society. The picture presented of them by the newspapers is therefore incorrect. The death squads are involved in stealing cars and freight, drug dealing, receiving stolen goods, extortion and other crimes.

● The crimes perpetrated by the death squads normally affect lower-income sections of the population. Both victims and death-squad collaborators are drawn from this section of society.

● Most of the victims of the death squads are not dangerous criminals. They are often innocent of any crime and are often killed for vengeance or the private motives of the financiers behind the death squads.

● The murders committed by the death squads do not have any salutary effect on the actions of street children and do not help to reduce crime. The stronger the death squad, the greater is its power to carry out the most diverse crimes without fear of punishment.

The Tenderine kidnapping and the publication of this manifesto were not in vain. Elected by the progressive forces of Pernambuco, Governor Arraes was obliged to respond to their pressure and order an investigation into the activities of the death squads. Names and facts were presented that proved the links between the death squads and organised crime. Among the people investigated was Xavier, accused of the death of Marcos Alexandre da Silva.

Cops and robbers

In the state of Mato Grosso do Sul, adolescents suspected of selling drugs were being eliminated by the death squads. The Federal police discovered that the killers were local policemen, yet it was far from being a 'clean up' operation, since the killers were themselves drug dealers, using police vehicles to deliver drugs. The victims were merely casualties in a battle for control of the local trade. In Manaus, drug dealers were also killed and the murders attributed to the death squads, until it was discovered that the death squads were also involved in drug dealing, taking advantage of the proximity of Colombia, Peru and Bolivia.

In Rio de Janeiro drug trafficking is believed to be controlled by the organisers of the illegal lottery, the *jogo de bicho* (animal game). They have the capital and organisation to deal in large quantities of drugs, which are sold by the *bicheiros* to local dealers who control the trade in their neighbourhood. The *bicheiros* enjoy enormous prestige in the community, winning respect and admiration for the financial support they give to local samba schools and for funding social services that the government is unable or unwilling to provide. They also have solid contacts with the police.

In this vast web of crime, it is difficult to distinguish between criminal and law enforcer. Although the Justice Ministers of Brazil's states have amassed information on police corruption, some of them admit that their information is far from complete. It is extremely difficult for internal investigations to progress since corporate loyalty within the police force protects any officer who might be accused. The police feel that they are badly paid and are therefore

Rio.

justified in making extra cash by protecting criminals or sponsoring crime. It is a short step from that to working alongside gangs in the planning and execution of crimes and the elimination of rivals. They know they can always put the blame for any assassination on the death squads, who are supported by the community and tolerated by local police forces. 'There's no doubt about it. The police force is getting more and more rotten right across the country. It is one of the public services that has deteriorated most', believes Amazonino Mendes, Governor of the state of Amazonas. When Amazonino was elected, he regularly received information about the involvement of police in organised crime, especially in car theft and drug dealing. 'I gave them a period of grace in which to change their ways, but they never changed at all', he remembers.

In 1987, four children were murdered after being accused of burgling the house of a former police chief in Amazonas. The bodies disappeared but were later found. Preliminary investigations revealed that plain clothes policemen, including Inspector Eliseu Montarroyos, were responsible for the murders. Soon after, the journalist Luiz Octavio Monteiro, who had information on how the death squads functioned in Manaus, was murdered. Fellow journalists say the death squads got rid of Monteiro before he could publish what he knew. The same happened to Mario Eugênio, a journalist who worked on the *Correio Brasiliense* and to Maria Nilce, a columnist who worked in Espírito Santo. A few days before she was killed, she had written about the participation of Espírito Santo's *bicheiros* in the drug trade.

Amazonino made an unexpected move. He abolished the *polícia civil*, the civilian police force in charge of organising the fight against crime, and made the uniformed *polícia militar* responsible for all law enforcement. In response, several sadistic crimes were committed, which Amazonino was told were carried out by ex-members of the *polícia civil* to hit back at the Governor. His domestic life was affected when he started to receive anonymous telephone messages threatening his children, driving his wife into a state of panic. 'If they had wanted to, they would have killed me. I know what these people are capable of', says Amazonino.

On 15 July 1989, there was a rare case of a death squad being caught red-handed. The place was Rio de Janeiro and the group was led by Pedro Capeta, accused by Volmer do Nascimento of working for the death squads. The police turned up shortly after the group had arrived at the home of Edson Carvalho Policarpo, known as 'Gordinho', whom they accused of theft. The death squad, six men in all, were in two cars. Four were off-duty police and two were employed by the Justice Department, including João Alberto Neves Buelho, Pedro Capeta's son. Two of the group were said to be professional killers. Gordinho got wind of their arrival and so had time to escape across the roof-tops. When his mother screamed and begged for mercy, one of the death squad shouted, 'Shut your mouth, you whore.'

This time though, a police patrol appeared and called in reinforcements. There was a shoot-out which ended in the death-squad members being arrested. Pedro Capeta, leader of the group, arrived shortly afterwards and was also arrested. The police arrived just as the members of the group were ransacking the house. They had already made a large pile of booty on the floor. The police later discovered that a shopkeeper had paid the group to kill Gordinho. Inspector Elson Campelo commented, 'This case shows how hollow are the claims that the death squads in Rio de Janeiro only kill crooks. The fact is that they are groups of murderers who kill for money and steal the belongings of their victims.'

Police brutality

It is rare for any of the abused children to publicly accuse their torturers. However, cases of torture are so common that there are more and more exceptions. On 19 January, 1988, Max Mauro, Governor of Espírito Santo, a state notorious for the involvement of its police in organised crime, was on a 'walkabout' in a poor neighbourhood called Itanhenga, on the outskirts of Vitória. He received a surprise when Gilson Carlos Soledad, 11 years old, managed to duck the security men and asked the Governor for a chat.

The security men tried to cut in, but the Governor asked the boy what he wanted. Gilson told him that the previous month he had been beaten up by the police in Campo Grande in the municipality of Cariacica. 'I jumped over into the neighbour's yard to drink some water. As I was leaving, a passing policeman saw me and began to hit me', he explained. The Governor and his advisers watched in silence as the boy lifted his shirt to reveal clear marks on his wrists and ankles. He said he had been handcuffed and had his legs tied together at the ankles while the police hit him. 'Do you know who it was?' asked the Governor. 'I could recognise him', replied Gilson. However, Gilson later admitted that it might be difficult because the injuries to his eyes were so serious that he now had difficulty seeing. 'He nearly blinded me. His boots were steel-tipped and he kicked me in the face', he said.

The name of the policeman in question was never discovered, just as the whereabouts of the torture centres in Vitória described by children who had been arrested were never discovered. The human rights organisations, the Brazilian Lawyers' Order and the Movement of Street Children all presented documents to the authorities describing the torture and denouncing the police practice of extorting bribes in exchange for releasing children from custody; to no avail.

Despite the dangers, there are other boys willing to both identify themselves and their attackers, 'I am no longer afraid of denouncing the police who torture street children. They can beat me up, kill me but I will carry on denouncing them', says Ely Andes, 16 years old. His whole body bears the signs of torture and there is a scar running right across his forehead. His story shows just how violent the police can be. Ely used to live in Vitória, where in May 1988 he accused Radio Patrol Car 245 of extortion. He claimed that men in that patrol had demanded a share of the spoils of , and the Children's Pastoral Service prepared a document

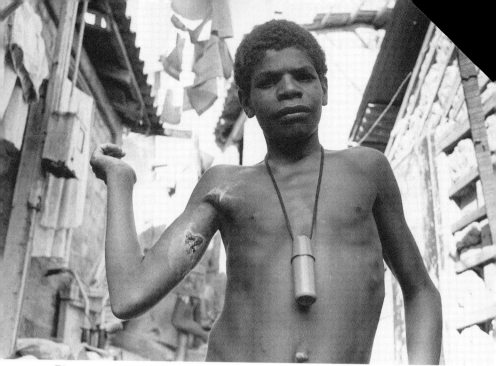

Rio.

setting out the details of the case. Two months later the police had their vengeance. They were especially tough on Ely to intimidate anybody else who might dare to follow his example.

Ely was kidnapped by the same policemen he had accused and taken to Morro da Fonte Grande, a place that the police in Vitória often use to torture their victims. 'After hitting me with a club, they made me kneel down and the sergeant started to cut my hair with a hunting knife. I asked him not to because he might cut my head, but he carried on. Then, I felt a cut in my forehead and blood gushing out', says Ely, showing the scar on his forehead. 'They carried on beating me up for two hours or so even after they had wounded me with the knife', he continues.

He was left at the side of a road, found by another policeman and taken to a police station before finally being allowed to go home. After such a traumatic experience, he preferred to stay indoors for several days because he was afraid of being murdered, but after a few days decided to go to school. It was not a good idea. Ely says he was approached by Radio Patrol Car 128 and, once more, taken to Morro da Fonte Grande. 'I was handcuffed, tied up, beaten and threatened with death several times', he says. He demonstrates how a sergeant put a gun to his head and told him he would kill him if

...entioned anything about what had happened. 'But he didn't
count on me shooting my mouth off again', he adds defiantly.

A.G. Lewis, 13, said to be a 'dangerous juvenile delinquent', was
arrested in 1987. His nickname was Faísca (Speedy). He accuses the
policeman, Herval Neves, of beating him up in the police children's
department. All fairly routine, but Faísca had a bullet in his leg.
He had been shot several weeks earlier by police who tried to catch
him without success and his leg was swollen and festering where
the bullet had entered. 'I asked them to take me to a hospital but
they refused. I wanted the bullet extracted from my leg', he says.
Instead they hit him and kicked him on the very place of the bullet
wound.

Carlos Bezerra of the National Movement of Street Children
believes that many policemen are actually unbalanced and need
psychiatric treatment. One particular case made a deep impression
on him. A mentally ill boy who lived in Anderson Street, Rio de
Janeiro, used to walk up and down Cinelandia, a street in the centre
of Rio. Every night, the police used to kick and harass him. They
used to pour glue in his hair. This went on for month after month,
until the boy would run, screaming at the top of his voice, every
time he saw a policeman.

One day, in an unexpected act of defiance, 'Anderson' spat in the
face of one of the policemen. Other policemen surrounded him. His
face full of terror, he tried to escape, but he couldn't. Taking a razor
from his pocket, he slashed the face of the nearest policeman, and
was beaten up all the more for his troubles. 'Can you imagine how
desperate this boy must have been to take on a group of policemen
with a razor?' asks Carlos.

Police extortion

During our research, we found dozens of children and educators
from all over Brazil willing to put on record that the police
themselves are encouraging children to commit crimes. If the child
does not give part of the proceeds to the police, he or she is detained.
In Recife, Ana Lira, a teacher and FUNABEM adviser who used to
work in the police children's department, has conducted several
pieces of research on juvenile crime. On one occasion, she asked the
children she interviewed what they would most like to be. The
results surprised her: 30 per cent said they would like to join the
police. Ana Lira taped a conversation with 'Amanda', 9, who had
been arrested several times for theft. 'Why would you like to join

the police?', she asked. 'So I could steal without getting caught', came the reply.

The police authorities excuse this kind of extortion by claiming it is caused by lack of training and low wages. A policeman in Brazil earns, on average, the equivalent of three minimum wages. An officer in charge of a police station earns the equivalent of about six minimum wages. A police chief, who asked to remain anonymous, said, 'I know that it is no excuse, but this is the root of the problem. How can you expect exemplary conduct from a policeman who does not earn enough money to pay the rent or buy meat for his family? It is obvious that the low level of wages can only lead to corruption. It is to be expected that he sells protection for cash. And, of course, it is the children on the streets that are most open to this kind of abuse.' Hélio Saboya, head of the Justice Department in Rio de Janeiro, and a former human rights activist, adds 'It is impossible to have a good policeman in a rotten country.'

The Children's Pastoral Service in Duque de Caxias prepared a dossier of statements made by victims and witnesses of violence. For obvious reasons, the names of the people who made the statements were omitted from the dossier. These statements frequently mention extortion. In statement no. 2 of the dossier, a 14-year-old boy says, 'The police threaten me, they tell me to steal for them. If I don't steal anything for them, they say they are going to kill me.' In statement no. 7, a 13 year old says, 'He [the policeman] hit me hard; when I have money on me, he tells me to give it to him, he tells me to go and steal for them. Once one of them came up to me in the shopping centre and questioned me. He took 500 *cruzados* from me. I only had 500 *cruzados* on me to buy a packet of biscuits to eat at work. The policeman took my 500 *cruzados* and told me to go and steal something else for him. I didn't tell anybody because I was afraid of getting shot.'

Death squads and politics

Some death-squad leaders have tried to extend their influence into the political field, where they are feared because of the private armies they control. Pedro Capeta, for example, is a member of the *Partido Trabalhista Brasileira*, the Brazilian Labour Party (PTB), in Duque de Caxias. Volmer do Nascimento accuses the deputy mayor of Duque de Caxias, José Carlos Lacerda, of administering the payments made to the private security firms that act as a cover for the operations of the death squads. Lacerda denies this, while admitting that he employs the private security firms because the police are not able to cope with the level of crime.

In São Bernardo, Esquerdinha was a candidate for the Christian Democrat Party (PDC) in the local council elections, but was strongly opposed by the *Partido dos Trabalhadores*, Workers Party (PT), which has consistently denounced his clandestine activities. When a seminar was organised on the subject of violence, Dalmas Santos, a judge, was invited to speak. Esquerdinha's activities were inevitably going to come up in discussion. In the middle of the debate, Esquerdinha came in, coughed ostentatiously and calmly sat down to listen. The crowd froze and some of those present contributed nothing further to the discussion.

In the 1988 elections, the PT and community leaders in the poor neighbourhoods claimed that the death squads were being hired by other political parties to help with their campaigns and intimidate their rivals.

Students of violence consulted during the preparation of this book said they had no doubt that, with time, these groups will become more politicised and will end up creating power systems similar to those organised by the *bicheiros* and drug dealers in Rio de Janeiro. The controllers of these areas make their own laws and maintain private armies. The police usually avoid entering their areas. 'It is like a person who buys a lion cub for his home. At the beginning, the cub is no problem, but it goes on growing. Nobody will burgle the house, of course, but the owner is going to end up as frightened as the thief', says the sociologist and senator, Fernando Henrique Cardoso. The senator has asked for a special parliamentary commission to be set up to investigate the death squads.

5

Supporting murder

In addition to enjoying official protection, death squads and police who abuse their power are often supported by the general public. Leaders of human rights movements accept that it is difficult to win public support for the fight against police and death-squad outrages. Large sections of the population are so frightened by the increase in street crime, that they will support any attempt to deal with the problem. Their fears are whipped up by the press, especially the crime programmes on the radio. These are sensationalist programmes, full of 'news' stories that have been either invented or exaggerated. They have a large audience among the poorer sections of the community, bringing prestige and credibility to the people who present them. One presenter, Afanásio Jazadji, was elected state congressman in 1986 with the highest number of votes cast for that position in the history of Brazil. Jazadji has spoken out in favour of the torture and extermination of 'criminals'.

There is certainly no shortage of material for the radio programmes. In 1989, 50,029 crimes involving theft, break-ins, muggings, armed robbery and murder were recorded in São Paulo alone. In Rio de Janeiro it was even worse: from January to November 1989, according to Justice Department statistics, a murder was committed every hour; there were 61 robberies a day; eight pickpocketing incidents every minute; and 123 stolen cars a day. These are just the recorded crimes — half the victims do not report the incident, showing the general lack of confidence in the police force. Some crimes, especially the less serious ones such as pickpocketing, are committed by minors. The statistics show that most murders and armed robberies are committed by adults, though the number of children implicated is increasing. Because of this, public support for the war against street children has grown.

In most of the big cities there is a small, isolated, and disorganised group of people willing to protest at the ill-treatment of street children. The people involved do not have the means to publicise their views widely, but the press occasionally publishes articles on the subject. Even then, they have little effect on public opinion. In September 1989, the *Folha de São Paulo* gave headline treatment to the massacre of children, detailing the numbers involved, and kept up the news coverage for four days. Readers expressed some degree of outrage, especially when the foreign press, alerted by the *Folha*, went to Brasília to cover a protest in which children unfurled banners with the names of the murder victims. Although one or two State Justice Ministers protested their innocence and the then Minister of Justice, Saulo Ramos, promised to take action, within a few days the matter was forgotten and the middle-class view once again held sway. The defence of juvenile 'delinquents' was portrayed more as an attack on decent people's rights to walk down the street in safety.

Jairo Gonçalves, lawyer and legal adviser to the Church's Pastoral Service for Children in São Paulo, and a participant in several human rights organisations, is tired of hearing the same old questions: 'Why do you defend criminals? Don't you think that we are better rid of these people? Shouldn't they be in prison?' Jairo tries to explain the principles of equal rights for all though usually with little success. 'Suspicion falls on the kids in the street, whether they are criminals or not. It's enough for a child to be dressed in ragged clothes for someone to think that he is going to steal their wallet. These kids are as feared as they are visible. Even if they are selling bubble gum, lemons or anything else on the street, they are still suspect', explains Jairo. In Pernambuco, this distrust led to a boy being arrested for 'suspected lewd thoughts'.

Cases of torture made a big impact on the public during the military dictatorship (1964-85) when the victims were political prisoners. Today, torture continues to take place regularly both in police stations and on the streets, yet provokes only mild indignation. The public's main worry is demonstrated clearly by its heavy investment in all kinds of security apparatus for their homes and cars. An increasing number of people are acquiring their own arms, a further sign of declining public confidence in the police.

A shop-owner who helps to maintain a death squad on the outskirts of São Paulo justified himself by saying, 'Nobody wants the kids to get killed. The problem is that there is no other solution. If they get arrested, the courts just let them go and they are free to

Salvador, Bahia.

steal again. And my shop continues to be under threat. Don't I have the right to run my shop in peace?.'

This line of reasoning is common among businessmen, who all complain about the lack of security. Some of them finance the work of the death squads; others employ policemen or former policemen to look after the security of their business. It is common to hear stories of torture being carried out on the premises of these businesses. 'We are receiving an increasing amount of information about ill-treatment inside the shops. The shops end up serving as torture chambers', says Rita Célia Gouveia, a lawyer who works with young people in Salvador for the Brazilian Lawyers Order. In Bahia, one boy was paralysed after being beaten up in a supermarket belonging to the Paes Mendonca chain, according to a formal complaint made by the OAB. The boy's family wants compensation but the supermarket will not admit responsibility.

'The truth is that we are seeing the creation of private militias in this country and I fear that they will soon be out of control', says Hélio Bicudo, head of Legal Affairs at the São Paulo city administration. As a result there are areas in the big cities where it is like living in the wild west. Bicudo says that, at least in São Paulo city, the death squads have been eliminated, but the police force itself has carried on where the death squads stopped and it kills with total impunity. As evidence, he points out that for every 600 'delinquents' killed in São Paulo, there are 20 police fatalities, whereas the ratio in the United States is three to one. 'Society at large is in favour of exterminating them', believes Bicudo. In the 1970s, he came into the public eye over his virtually single-handed and successful campaign against the São Paulo death squads.

Some communities make their support for the death squads very clear. In 1988, in Vitória, a public controversy erupted when it emerged that the police were picking up children from the streets, beating them up, taking them down to São Paulo or Rio de Janeiro and throwing them on the streets there. A commission of inquiry was set up by the Espírito Santo state legislative assembly and the policemen concerned were suspended, but they were ardently defended in some quarters. Many of the boys being 'deported' by the police lived in Vila Rubim, a neighbourhood in the centre of the city where the shopkeepers were angry at the lack of security. They demanded immediate measures from the Governor, Max Mauro, and publicly threatened to take justice into their own hands if necessary. 'These little scoundrels are criminals and I don't care how old they are', declared Aristidis Constantinidis, then President of the Shopkeepers Association. His vice-president, Devenir Brito Ferreira, was more explicit. He said that shopkeepers were ready to solve the problem once and for all, even if it meant using 'unconventional methods'. 'We don't care what it takes to solve this problem', he warned. When the human rights movement, the street children's movement and the Catholic Church all condemned this public incitement to violence, the president of the Espírito Santo Federation of Commerce issued a press release, saying, 'If the Catholic Church is so worried about this type of people, then let them house them in their convents and monasteries and turn them into saints.'

Fernando da Silva Ramos was killed in Diadema on the outskirts of São Paulo, on 27 August 1987. Like so many children, Fernando was murdered by the police, but this case was different. It received national and international attention because Fernando was the star of Hector Babenco's film *Pixote*, in which he played the role of a juvenile delinquent. The attention generated by the case led to the suspension of the police officers involved and a public investigation which revealed that Fernando had been complaining of police harassment and death threats ever since he had appeared in the film. It was alleged, as usual, that he died in an exchange of fire, yet his body had six bullet holes from shots fired from above. In other words, he was shot while lying on the floor or kneeling. A witness heard Pixote plead, 'Don't kill me. I have got a daughter to bring up.' Even after these details came to light, the police received bouquets of flowers from the people and shopkeepers of Diadema. Banners saying 'Pixote was a crook. The people are grateful to the police' appeared in the streets.

Crime and punishment

Even those reformers who have tried to improve the appalling conditions in children's institutions have aroused public anger and seen their reputations tarnished. One former director of the Foundation for the Social Welfare of Minors in the State of Bahia, the lawyer Itana Viana, suffered a constant stream of criticism over her efforts at reform. She eventually had to leave her job at the Foundation even though she had been nominated by the then Governor, Waldir Pires, usually sensitive to the demands of the human rights movement. Slowly but surely, political support for Itana drained away.

One initiative which caused consternation among the Bahian elite was prompted by a report showing the incidence of AIDS among the minors in her care. Itana decided to distribute condoms, provoking a public uproar in the middle of which the head of the Child Protection Service, Jefet Eustáquio, decided to open an inquiry and accused Itana of encouraging 'promiscuous behaviour among minors'. Conservative sectors of the press insinuated that she was stealing from the Foundation and called for her to be sacked.

Itana's most unpopular decision came after visiting the Agricultural-Industrial School for Minors in Maragojipe, in the interior of the state of Bahia. Children who had murdered entire families were sent there, but so were children who had been found guilty of stealing an orange. Itana was shocked by what she saw there. The children lived behind bars, the toilets were blocked up, many of the beds were in close proximity to these toilets, there was dust everywhere and the kitchen was infested with rats and cockroaches. None of the showers worked. She found out that the inmates, many of whom had spent years in Maragojipe, were subjected to the most varied kinds of torture, yet nobody had tried to do anything for them. 'I didn't consult anyone', admits Itana. 'I closed the place. It wasn't a place fit for human beings. If anyone wants to re-open it, that's up to them.' Hounded by the Bahian elite, who called her 'mad' and 'subversive', Itana left her job. However,

after all the revelations nobody had the courage to re-open Maragojipe prison. At least Itana has the pleasure of this one victory.

Clearing the streets

Since state governors know that personal security is one of the main worries of the general population, they are increasingly using the 'dragnet' tactic of clearing the streets of the major cities. Any 'suspicious-looking' children are arrested and taken to the police children's department. In 1988, the Rio police children's department detained 1,375 minors for vagrancy. This number rose to 2,052 in 1989.

In Manaus there is a proliferation of gangs of juvenile thieves, known locally as *galeras*, who sometimes take over whole neighbourhoods. People are demanding action, and Governor Amazonino Mendes has lost points in the opinion polls because of the growth of the *galeras*. Under pressure, he has promised to get rid of them, although he has yet to explain exactly how. His provisional response has been to remove every child from the streets in what has become known as 'Operation Vacuum Cleaner'. Anybody who was not in the gangs before is now just one step away from joining one of them. 'I admit that I don't know what do about it. These children need schools and jobs. But we haven't got enough schools or jobs', says Amazonino.

In Rio de Janeiro, in 1989, the beach suburbs were declared a 'maximum security zone', and dozens of soldiers were ferried in to support the army of private security men. Any poor-looking child was picked up and taken to the police station. The then coordinator of the National Movement of Street Children, Maria Tereza Moura, protested to the police chiefs, arguing that it was inadmissible to ban children from going near the beach areas just because the police suspected they might commit a crime. After several fruitless meetings with the police, one of them confided, 'You are right about this. But we cannot do a thing. There is a lot of pressure being put on us from higher up. And I can tell you, the pressure is strong.' Governor Moreira Franco was being leant on by the powerful Hotel Owners Association, which feared that Rio de Janeiro's violent image was starting to damage the tourist trade. Young boys walking along the hotel fronts had become associated with muggings and theft, and many of the boys walking around the area were indeed thieves.

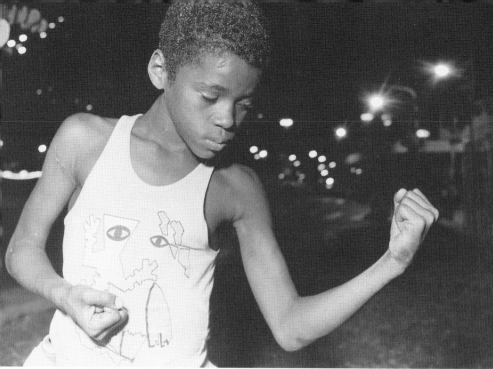

Recife.

A recent phenomenon in Rio de Janeiro is that of the *anjos da guarda* (guardian angels). The 'angels' are middle-class people trained in martial arts who have formed a uniformed private army with the objective of dealing out justice to criminals who operate around the city's beaches. They enjoy the support and even admiration of bathers, chasing after muggers to overpower them and hand them over to the police. As might be expected, the 'angels' commit their share of arbitrary acts, yet the Rio middle classes are no more shocked by the guardian 'angels' than by the 'clean-up' operations. This way of dealing with juvenile delinquency has produced an informal apartheid system in which a certain type of person is banned from going to particular places.

In one of these 'clean-ups', in January 1989, 23 children were taken to the police children's department, but only nine later reappeared. Nobody knows what happened to the others. 'I would just like to see how the country would react if 14 doctors had disappeared, or 14 police officers, or 14 journalists', says Maria Tereza Moura. In today's Brazil if a single journalist was arrested for whatever motive and tortured in the police station, there would be a national scandal, yet during the research for this book, we heard dozens of statements detailing torture and ill-treatment of prisoners. Some of the people interviewed experience torture as a routine daily occurrence. 'Since when has a journalist been worth more than anybody else?' asks Maria. 'Is the torture of a young poor boy supposed to hurt less than the torture of a political intellectual?'

6

The law of silence

People working with street children defy the law of silence at great personal risk. The climate of fear makes it difficult to carry out official investigations or even to obtain more precise figures on the numbers of murders. When one former employee of the police children's department in Recife demanded details on the deaths of street children and named a few names, the telephone threats soon started. 'Look, you old whore, you had better keep your mouth shut.' At first, she ignored them, thinking that the callers lacked the courage to act. Early one morning, a caller warned, 'I've got good news for you. Three of your street children have been eliminated. You will see it in the paper today.'

It was true, but the woman faced even harder times ahead. Her daughter was kidnapped for several hours — the killers drove her around for a time, but then let her go when the Governor, Miguel Arraes, intervened directly. To see her daughter so traumatised and suffering from constant nightmares was too much for the woman. She stopped trying to expose the death squads and will only give interviews on the express condition that her name is not published. At that time, the Head of the Pernambuco Police, João Arraes, also promised to take on the death squads. Throughout the next week he received telephone calls: there was no talking, just the sound of machine-gun fire. 'It must be police officers who are doing this', he told the press.

According to the human rights organisation, IBASE, the death squads in Pernambuco are responsible for 57 per cent of the murders of children, an even higher proportion than in Rio de Janeiro. Desperate parents have painted protests such as 'Don't kill my children' on Pernambuco's street walls.

'Don't kill my kids. Who is to blame?' Recife.

In July 1989, the radio presenter Paulo Dias was kidnapped in Recife. In his programme he had been demanding a full investigation into the activities of the death squads. 'I went through two and a half hours of extreme tension', he recalls. He was overpowered by four armed men and driven off in a white Chevette with concealed number plates. While driving around deserted streets, they told him, 'Pray because you are going to die. Go on, pray.' Luckily he was more useful to the death squads alive than dead, since they only wanted to intimidate him and thereby intimidate others. They gave Paulo Dias a message: the next one to be kidnapped would be J. Menezes, another radio presenter who had asked for the full force of the law to be used against the death squads.

Members of the death squads know that they can go about their business with virtually no interference from the authorities, but there are limits. From time to time, protests force the local Governor to take action. Measures are sometimes taken, though most of them are soon bogged down in interminable committee meetings. During the governorship of Leonel Brizola in Rio de Janeiro, a commission was set up to investigate the death squads, after a ballerina accused her former lover, a police officer, of being a death-squad member.

After a year's delay, the investigation into 184 cases continued during the governorship of Moreira Franco. The members of the commission complained of the lack of police support for the investigation, saying they were not even given the money necessary to cover the costs of protecting witnesses. Most of the suspected members of the death squads were absolved but 23 people were found guilty and sentenced.

Three months prior to the kidnapping of Paulo Dias, the death squads carried out one of their most daring operations when they kidnapped Luís Tenderine, president of the Pernambuco Justice and Peace Commission. The action was a direct challenge to the Catholic Church, to which the Commission belongs. Tenderine was not only kidnapped, he was tortured for good measure. 'The kidnappers showed no signs of tension. They weren't on drugs. They were completely sure of themselves and what they were doing', recalls Tenderine.

Born in Italy, Tenderine had lived in Brazil for 20 years and had been actively involved in the labour and human rights movement before taking up the presidency of the Justice and Peace Commission in 1988. The Commission had for some time been denouncing the crimes of the death squads, yet even though the Governor, Miguel Arraes, and the head of his Justice Department, Almeida Filho, had shown sympathy for the Commission's cause, they had not taken concrete measures to combat the death squads. Tenderine decided to step up the pressure and gave an interview to the local press, after which the *Jornal do Comercio* ran the headline, 'Justice and Peace want the death squads punished.'

Tenderine started to receive anonymous telephone calls. The first said, 'You had better be careful. You must be very fond of your children.' Talking after the kidnapping, Tenderine said, 'To tell you the truth, I didn't attach a lot of importance to the calls. Previous presidents of the Commission have had to put up with the same thing.' This time, however, things were different. At 9.30pm one Saturday evening, two men approached Tenderine while he was sitting in his parked car. One of them, holding a gun, got into the driving seat; the other got into the back seat. They quickly removed Tenderine's spectacles. Tenderine protested that he was the president of the Justice and Peace Commission to which the kidnappers replied, 'We are also in the justice business. But we have got our own way of doing things.'

They drove Tenderine around deserted roads while repeatedly burning him with cigarette ends, especially in his face. Then the car stopped and the men said, 'You can get out here. This is a warning to you and the Church to stop asking for an investigation.' One of Tenderine's kidnappers had earlier explained, 'We are not going to kill you because you have such close links with the Church and we know that you would become a martyr. We have no intention of creating a martyr.'

He was left naked at the roadside and had to seek help on foot. Although the kidnapping was a traumatic experience for the President of the Justice and Peace Commission, it helped the fight against the death squads by putting further pressure on the Governor to act. A Movement for Life was set up, supported by all the popular movements in Pernambuco, which insisted that Miguel Arraes treat the question as a priority. He established a special inquiry into the death squads, but the murders continued. Some death squads were broken up, but not before some of their members were killed by their fellow assassins, fearful that interrogation would lead them to divulge the names of others involved.

Secret cemeteries

During such periods, the death squads adopt a lower profile. To keep their actions out of the news, they bury their victims in secret cemeteries and threaten their families with trouble if they talk. Many relatives are too frightened even to report the murders. Since 1989, when the killing of street children began to receive publicity in the national and international press, Rio de Janeiro's more experienced crime reporters have noticed how much rarer it has become to see the bodies of young death-squad victims lying in the street or in ditches at the roadside, although this still happens in the case of murdered adults. Reporters remember one occasion when a murdered child lay in a street of Greater Rio de Janeiro for more than a month.

In 1989 journalists of the French magazine *L'Express* came to Brazil to report on the extermination of street children. In Duque de Caxias, they interviewed the then chief police officer, Henrique Pinheiro Alves. During the interview, Alves labelled juvenile delinquents as 'monsters'. When questioned about the existence of secret cemeteries, he grew furious, 'It's the communists linked to the bishop who put these rumours about. That Dom Mauro Morelli, who fornicates with the people in his charge, is to blame. He should shut up.' Alves went on to call the bishop an 'imbecile'. The reporters claimed they managed to persuade police officers of the 59th brigade of Duque de Caxias to take them to a secret cemetery, an enormous ditch about five metres deep. One of them asked their guides, 'Are there any innocent people in there?' 'All of them are innocent', came the reply. The reporter asked if there were any children buried there. The police officer coldly answered that the children 'were more dangerous than the adults.'

When the bishop of Duque de Caxias, Dom Mauro Morelli, heard about Henrique Alves' outburst, he decided that Alves must have something to do with the anonymous telephone calls he had been receiving, calls that had included threats to Volmer do Nascimento. 'These statements are calculated to encourage the death squads to attack me. If anything happens to me, I will hold the person who employs Alves, Governor Moreira Franco, responsible', declared Dom Mauro.

Volmer do Nascimento had argued with this same police officer, when they met by chance in the street and Alves started to criticise the work of the Children's Pastoral Service. According to Volmer, Alves was very aggressive, 'I shall finish up putting you on trial for the corruption of children', he said. 'What do you mean?', asked Volmer. 'It is very easy to get thrown into jail here', replied Alves. At one point the police offered Volmer their protection, either through two guards at the front of his house or a firearm to use in his own defence. He refused both alternatives, saying, 'I don't know how to shoot. And if I was to be attacked, they would have the excuse they need to kill me. And to put two police officers outside my house is like putting the fox to guard the hens.'

There are few people in Brazil who have both the reputation and the political cover necessary to stand up to the death squads, and there is no pressure to investigate their crimes. Many of those who dare to name names are threatened or attacked. Since 1983, when investigations into the death squads in Rio de Janeiro began, 13 witnesses have been murdered. At least one witness saw death-squad members circulating freely in the building where statements were being taken from the witnesses.

One person who 'knew too much' was Sister Ana Maria in São Bernardo. She claims to have witnessed a cold-blooded murder by the best-known death-squad member of the region, Esquerdinha. In January 1988, in the neighbourhood of Parque das Esmeraldas, Sister Ana Maria saw a *polícia civil* police car draw up outside the house of a young man supposedly guilty of a series of crimes. According to the Sister, the police, led by Esquerdinha, took the boy out of the house and shot him in front of his mother, as she begged them to let him go. Sister Ana wrote an unsigned description of this incident. 'I tried to find out something about the victim', she recalls.

'His family told me that he was mentally ill, that he had hospital documents to prove it. Unfortunately, we are forced to witness such horrible scenes as this. The boy was killed in front of his mother.'

Thereafter, Sister Ana was the target of repeated harassment. At the beginning of April 1988, as she was talking to some friends in the street, some of Esquerdinha's group appeared, flaunting their guns. 'I started to walk down the road. I had taken about ten steps when one of them fired a shot into the air', says Sister Ana. 'I stopped a moment. When I started to walk again, there was another shot. They spent the whole day walking up and down the streets near my house. They also always made a point of showing the Sisters in my community that they were armed, as if guns were toys.'

Sister Ana lived in constant fear of being shot or kidnapped. On 13 June that same year, she was at a fair organised by her community with the support of the church. At the end of the fair, as they were beginning to tidy the place up, one of Esquerdinha's group came up to her and asked her if she would go and help somebody who had just been taken ill. Suspicious, she refused. 'I can't', she said. 'I've run out of petrol.' 'We'll fill your tank', came the reply. Some of her friends warned her not to go in any circumstances and that she should leave the fair as quickly as possible. They advised her to sleep in a friend's house. 'I left immediately with the other Sisters. We came back on the following day and saw that the same person who had approached me passed in front of the house several times.'

When Sister Ana decided to tell the authorities about this intimidation, the chief judge of São Bernardo, Dalmas Santos, replied that little could be done about it. He admitted that he knew of Esquerdinha's activities but did not have the legal powers to press any charges. 'There are two options', Dalmas told Sister Ana, 'continue in the same situation or begin an investigation in the certain knowledge that you will be killed on the next street corner.'

Expedito Soares, a local congressman elected by the Workers Party, had also warned people about Esquerdinha. In 1985, Expedito publicly criticised what he called the fragile security system in operation at the São Bernardo Town Hall. Soon afterwards, Esquerdinha telephoned him to give him some 'good news': he had killed a crook known as 'Tarzan'. Esquerdinha had been sitting in his car, with a machine gun on his lap, when he saw Tarzan coming along the street. Without a second thought, he got out of his car, went up to Tarzan and mowed him down with a burst of machine-gun fire. They found Tarzan's body a week later in a ravine.

Esquerdinha denies that he is part of a death squad, claiming that his political enemies have tried to tarnish his reputation. He admits he has lost count of the number of people he has killed, but claims he has only killed others during shoot-outs, 'I never intend to kill anybody. But I know that I don't want to die', he explains.

Sister Ana Maria did not want to die either, so the Church asked Governor Orestes Quércia to look into the case. He, in turn, asked the Justice Department to investigate. Father Agostinho of the Church's Prison Pastoral service, currently working in Ribeirão Preto in the interior of São Paulo state, decided to shadow the investigation closely. Before long he became suspicious of its slow progress and sought a meeting with an old friend who now had a high position in the police force. 'Why this delay?' asked Agostinho, 'Everybody knows who the guilty people are.' His friend appeared ill-at-ease and offered only feeble excuses, until in the end the police official gave his real opinion. 'Look, Agostinho', he said, 'the problem is that nobody really wants to complete the investigation. I would forget about it if I were you. When those people catch crooks, they are doing the police a favour.' The conversation left Agostinho convinced that Sister Ana was in greater danger than she imagined. She had continued to suffer intimidation from the death squads even after the investigation into their activities had got under way. She grew convinced that there was no means of protecting her personal security and today lives in Italy.

Fear on the streets

If governors, lawyers and clergy run into problems when trying to do something about death squads and police violence, what hope have the potential victims? Street children have no contacts in the press or the government. They do not even own the clothes that would allow them to walk into a government office. They are the ones who are most afraid and who therefore tend to keep quiet, creating a further obstacle to any investigation into the extermination and torture of young people by the police.

Children are all too familiar with the expression 'get rid of the evidence'. Because they live on the streets and in some cases are even recruited for criminal activity, they often know the names of the police officers and crooks involved in crime and death-squad activities. Although a local community is often relieved when ⸮ dead body of a young boy involved in petty crime is found or streets, in many cases the boy is simply the victim of gangs or policemen who think he knows too much.

It was nearly midnight, February, 1988, when there was a knock on the door of a house in a slum of Duque de Caxias. 'Open up, it's the police', said a voice. Maria Helena Mendes, frightened, opened the door to the 'police officers', who said that they had come to take her two sons, Fernando and Aldenir to the police children's department for questioning. After they had taken the boys by force, their mother, in desperation, called the neighbours and went with them to the police station. Just as she had feared, the boys were not there. She spent the night looking for her sons, but first thing in the morning, a neighbour, breathless, arrived with the bad news. She had spotted two charred and bullet-ridden bodies near her house. They were all that was left of Maria's sons.

Fernando and Aldenir had no criminal record. They both worked washing cars at a local garage. Nothing very dangerous on the face of it, but the garage was right in front of a police station and, according to their mother, their job made them constant witnesses of the comings and goings at the police station. They 'knew too much'.

In São Paulo state, a boy with precious information is now in hiding, paralysed and confined to a wheelchair. Along with another two boys, he was targeted by the death squads in his home town, São Bernardo, but managed to save himself by pretending to be dead. The other two were murdered. The boy's injuries left him permanently crippled. In September 1989 he attended a national meeting of street children, where he gave an interview to a journalist whose subsequent report mentioned that he was paralysed. Although the writer omitted his age or home town, the São Bernardo death squads identified him immediately and he had to flee and go to live in the interior of São Paulo state.

Something similar occurred in Pernambuco where, on 4 October 1989, Dário da Silva, 15, and Luís Adriano, 16, were kidnapped from their homes. Dário da Silva was dragged from the bedroom which he shared with his four younger brothers. His mother tried to stop the kidnapping but the men said that her son was the member of a criminal gang. The three kidnappers drove a white Volkswagen car and carried .12 calibre shotguns in an operation which bore the hallmark of the death squads. However, things did not go according to plan.

Dário's mother contacted the organisation called SOS Children, which promptly rang round all the police stations in Recife to try and locate Dário. They went to the head of the police children's department, who discovered that Dário was being held at the petty crime department with another eight boys, even though he was a minor. Dário was released and handed over to his mother. He was very frightened and was limping: his feet were badly injured.

Although Adriano's mother had assured SOS Children that Adriano was safe in the house of one of her friends, nine days after the kidnapping his bullet-ridden and tortured body was found. His friend Dário, victim and therefore witness of the kidnapping, now lives in fear for his own life. He knows it is no longer safe for him to live in Recife, but has nowhere to go in the interior of the state. Instead, the women of SOS Children have constantly to improvise hiding places for him — for how long, nobody can guess.

When 'Pingo', a boy from the neighbourhood of Peixinhos on the outskirts of Olinda, was kidnapped by members of the death squads, community leaders in the neighbourhood telephoned Roberto França, Secretary of the Justice Department and a respected activist in the human rights movement. França immediately put a call through to all police stations, demanding, 'Find this boy. I want him here straight away.' 'Pingo' was saved. According to his own testimony, his kidnappers had already put a plastic bag on his head ready to lead him to the side of the street to be shot. Now, he keeps himself well-hidden in Peixinhos to escape being recognised by death-squad members and killed to prevent him passing on the information he holds. 'Pingo' has lived to tell the tale, but says he will follow to the letter the implacable law of silence imposed by the underworld and never tell anybody the identity of his kidnappers.

'I get tired of seeing young boys arrive here with their bodies broken, scarred, bleeding, covered in bruises. You ask them what happened, who beat them up and so on and they tell you that they hurt themselves playing football. But we know very well that they have been beaten up by the police', says Rafael Indlenkofer, a 22-year-old German who left the pleasant city of Karlsruhe in Germany to come and work with the street children of north-east Brazil. Rafael stands out a mile in his blue jeans, t-shirt, leather sandals and with a ribbon in his hair. Each month, his friends in Germany, linked to the churches, send him a small amount of money on which he must live and pay the rent on a simple house in Recife. Rafael believes the boys know the names and even the nicknames of the people involved and where they operate from, but, 'they are scared to death of mentioning names. They know that if they do, they will have no protection. And they will have to face

Rafael Indlenkofer

the people they accuse out there in the streets. Nobody would be able to protect them from their fate.'

In Pernambuco, the police-controlled death squads are so well organised that they even have informers working inside FUNABEM. The informers work in FUNABEM's hostels and tell the death squads when their wards are discharged. Almeri Bezerra de Mello, President of FUNABEM in Pernambuco has strong suspicions about who the informers are, but can do little, 'An inquiry is necessary before a FUNABEM worker can be sacked. And to hold an inquiry, witnesses are needed. None of these boys will serve as a witness because they will be killed straight away', says Almeri, sadly.

Investigations usually bog down even when the accusers have the names of the people implicated, according to Carlos Bezerra of the National Movement of Street Children. In one case, a child was tortured in Rio de Janeiro's Cathedral. The policemen charged with the security of the building grabbed a boy who was walking near the cathedral, took him to their room, kicked him and threw ether in his eyes. Other boys rushed off to tell Carlos Bezerra who ran to the cathedral to find the boy writhing about, his eyes red and swollen. Carlos went straight to the head of the police and made an official complaint. An inquiry was opened and lasted six months, until Carlos asked the police officers in charge of the investigation to 'please' forget about it. One of the police officers agreed, 'It is not dangerous for you', he said, 'but they will take it out on the boy.'

The case was forgotten. It was lost among the hundreds of cases of violence committed daily against the children of our cities: violence in the police stations and violence on the street; violence from the security staff employed by private companies, who are under orders to keep street children away from the buildings of their employers. In all cases, the basic aim is to keep juvenile delinquents or potential delinquents as far away as possible. Murder is the inevitable result.

Resources and Action

Organisations campaigning on street children in Brazil

The Passage House is a refuge for some of the 30,000 young girls on the streets of Recife in north-east Brazil. A second refuge is currently being planned. In the UK, the Passage House is sponsored by WOMANKIND (Worldwide) which supports women's groups and organisations in developing countries, and CHILDHOPE UK, the UK branch of CHILDHOPE, an international movement for street children.

AMNESTY INTERNATIONAL campaigns against human rights abuse of Brazil's street children. An Amnesty report on the subject is available. In 1990 over 1,000 Amnesty members sent letters of support to Volmer do Nascimento, Rio de Janeiro coordinator of Brazil's National Movement of Street Children, following death threats against him and his children.

ANTI-SLAVERY INTERNATIONAL campaigns on issues of child labour and exploitation.

SAVE THE CHILDREN has recently opened an office in Recife to develop its work on Brazil.

STREETWISE INTERNATIONAL is a UK-based charity which aims to publicise the plight of children around the world and support groups working with them. It publishes a magazine, *Childlife*.

During 1991-2, Y-CARE INTERNATIONAL, the YMCA's world development agency, has a campaign called 'Pounding the Streets'. This aims to raise awareness among young people in Great Britain and Ireland about street children in developing countries and work that YMCAs are doing with them. An information pack is available.

Other aid agencies and organisations working on Brazil

OXFAM, CHRISTIAN AID and CAFOD address issues of urban and rural poverty and deprivation in Brazil.

BRAZIL NETWORK links individuals and organisations in the UK working on Brazil and interested in keeping up to date on events there. It publishes a quarterly newsletter.

Contact Addresses

UK

AMNESTY INTERNATIONAL
British Section
99-119 Rosebery Avenue
London EC1R 4RE

ANTI-SLAVERY
INTERNATIONAL
180 Brixton Road
London SW9 6AT

BRAZIL NETWORK
PO Box 1325
London SW9 0RA

CATHOLIC FUND FOR
OVERSEAS DEVELOPMENT
(CAFOD)
2 Romero Close
Stockwell Road
London SW9 9TY

CHILDHOPE UK
40 Rosebery Avenue
London EC1R 4RN

CHRISTIAN AID
PO Box 100
London SE1 7RT

OXFAM
274 Banbury Road
Oxford OX2 7DZ

SAVE THE CHILDREN FUND
17 Grove Lane
London SE5 8RD

STREETWISE
INTERNATIONAL
PO Box 58
Cambridge CB4 1EG

UNICEF-UK
55 Lincoln's Inn Fields
London WC2A 3NB

WOMANKIND
(WORLDWIDE)
122 Whitechapel High Street
London E1 7PT

Y-CARE INTERNATIONAL
640 Forest Rd
London E17 3DZ

USA

AMERICAS WATCH
Human Rights Watch
485 Fifth Avenue
New York NY 10017-6104

AMNESTY INTERNATIONAL
OF THE USA
322 8th Avenue
New York NY 10001

BRAZIL NETWORK
PO Box 2738
Washington DC 20013

CHILDHOPE USA
c/o US Committee for UNICEF
333 East 38th Street
New York
NY 10016

OXFAM AMERICA
114 Broadway
Boston
Massachussetts 02116

Further information on children

Peter Lee Wright, *Child Slaves*, Earthscan Publications, London, 1990

Annie Allsebrook and Anthony Swift, *Broken Promise*, Hodder & Stoughton, London, 1989

Caroline Moorehead (ed), *Betrayal: Child Exploitation in Today's World*, Barrie & Jenkins, London, 1989

Judith Ennew and Brian Milne, *The Next Generation: Lives of Third World Children*, Zed Books, London 1989

Further information on Brazil

There is an enormous range of reading matter on environmental issues and the Amazon basin, but accessible information on the country as a whole is relatively scarce:

Neil MacDonald, *Brazil: A Mask Called Progress*, Oxfam, Oxford, 1991

Brazil Network, *Trade Unions in Brazil: Fighting Back*, £1 including post and packing, Brazil Network, PO Box 1325, London SW9 0RA

Emir Sader and Ken Silverstein, *Without Fear of Being Happy: Lula, the Workers' Party and Brazil*, Verso, London, publication December 1991

For two vivid portraits of life in a *favela*, try:

Carolina Maria de Jesus, *Beyond All Pity*, first published by Souvenir Press, now in paperback with Earthscan, London, 1990

Alma Guillermoprieto, *Samba*, Bloomsbury, London, 1990

Amnesty International and Americas Watch produce regular human rights reports on Brazil. The most relevant to the problem of street children is:

Amnesty International, *Brazil: Torture and Extrajudicial Execution in Urban Brazil*, AI Index AMR 19/05/90, £2.30 (inc p&p)

Christian Aid distributes a video, *Same Rights for Severina* (25 minutes), discussing issues of inequality and human rights in Brazil. Free hire, or £9.99 purchase from Christian Aid's Marketing and Resources Department.

Further reading on Brazil from LAB

Fight for the Forest: Chico Mendes in his own words
Chico Mendes and Tony Gross

Chico Mendes, the charismatic founder of the Brazilian rubber tappers' union was murdered by a hired assassin on 22 December 1988.

In **Fight for the Forest**, Chico talks of his life's work in what was to be his last major interview. He recalls the rubber tappers' campaign against forest clearances and their alliances with local Indians and the international environmental lobby. Together, they developed sustainable alternatives for the Amazon which would guarantee both their livelihoods and the forest's future.

' ... an inspiring and chilling message.' David Bellamy in the *Observer*

1989   £4.75   96 pages   ISBN 0 906156 51 3

The Dance of the Millions: Latin America and the Debt Crisis
Jackie Roddick et al

This comprehensive account of the Latin American debt crisis includes case studies of Brazil, Peru and Costa Rica, examines the role played by the IMF and the World Bank, and considers the implications of the debt for future economic development in Latin America.

'A crisp and informative introduction to the Latin American debt crisis... clarity of presentation and a robust grasp of the structural characteristics of the world economy will ensure the success of this carefully reasoned polemic.' *Times Higher Education Supplement*

1988   £8.00   250 pages   ISBN 0 906156 30 0

New books from LAB

Faces of Latin America
Duncan Green

Five hundred years after Christopher Columbus' arrival in the Americas, Latin America still suffers from the legacy of the Conquest.

Faces of Latin America is a wide-ranging survey of the vital issues affecting Latin America today, including the environmental crisis, the role of the military and the burden of foreign debt.

Illustrated throughout with photos, eye-witness reports and testimony, **Faces of Latin America** analyses the roles of the main actors in the continent's history; both those in power and the poor majority who struggle for their vision of Latin America's future.

October 1991   £10.00   230 pages   ISBN 0 906156 59 9

Columbus: His Enterprise
Hans Koning

Who was Christopher Columbus? Fearless explorer or a man 'cruel in petty things... cruel on a continental scale'?

Columbus: His Enterprise describes the personality and motivation of a man who changed the course of history. Exploding the myth of the Great Navigator, the author reveals how Columbus accidentally found a continent and systematically pillaged its resources.

'Makes fascinating reading... should be compulsory.' Christopher Hill in the *New York Review of Books*

'The book is an idea that has finally found its time.' *Publishers Weekly*

June 1991   £5.75   142 pages   ISBN 0 906156 60 2

Published in the USA by Monthly Review Press, New York

Panama: Made in the USA
John Weeks and Phil Gunson

Explores the unanswered questions behind the US invasion of Panama in December 1989 and, reviewing the turbulent history of US-Panamanian relations, analyses the economic and geo-strategic importance of a country literally created by and for the US government.

'This is one of the finest investigations about American complicity in Latin America I have read. It is essential reading for anyone interested in the truth about the New World Order.' John Pilger

'A succinct and informed analysis of the US invasion, its background and its aftermath. The study could hardly be more timely, and the lessons more instructive.' Noam Chomsky

January 1991   £5.75   150 pages   ISBN 0 906156 55 6

The above prices are for paperback editions and include post and packing. Write for a complete list of LAB books to Latin America Bureau, 1 Amwell Street, London EC1R 1UL

LAB books are distributed in North America by Monthly Review Press, 122 West 27 Street, New York, NY10001.

LAB is a UK subscription agent for *Report on the Americas*, the largest English language magazine covering the region, published by the North American Congress on Latin America (NACLA) in New York. Write to LAB for details.

Index

The Latin America Bureau is a small, independent, non-profit-making research organisation established in 1977. LAB is concerned with human rights and related social, political and economic issues in Central and South America and the Caribbean. We carry out research and publish books, publicise and lobby, and work with Latin American and Caribbean support groups. We also brief the media, run a small documentation centre and produce materials for teachers.